Cynthia Wallace provides one
and compelling explanations o
I have read. She sheds light on
where too often rhetoric and half-truths have obscured the
legal and historic right of the Jewish people to a homeland.
Nations and individuals need to know the history before
they make historic decisions. Wallace provides it. I believe
it's a profound contribution to the world-wide dialogue
that should be read by diplomats, journalists and decision
makers as they deliberate on the pressing issue of our time.
—CHRIS MITCHELL
CBN NEWS MIDDLE EAST BUREAU CHIEF
JERUSALEM

Dr. Cynthia Wallace has put together a most important book on the foundational rights for Israel's existential privilege in Jerusalem and the land once known
as "Palestine". These foundational rights extend beyond
just 'humanitarian' considerations, being firmly moored
in the underpinnings of international law. This book
should be required reading for political representatives
and concerned citizens of any nation that desires to justly
pursue resolution of the seemingly unending territorial disputes between Israel and the Palestinians. While
Dr. Wallace's contribution does not pretend to be a "road
map for peace", without the relevant legal comprehension
there can be no "road map for peace".
—JOHNNY ENLOW
AUTHOR: THE SEVEN MOUNTAIN PROPHECY AND
THE SEVEN MOUNTAIN MANTLE

As we pray for God's ancient, firstborn People, the Jews,
and for the peace of Jerusalem, it is important that we also
understand the international legal foundations underlying
the key issues at stake. Dr. Cynthia Wallace, who personally
is deeply rooted in Scripture, has as well a long academic
career in international law. She has provided the global
community a most valuable and extremely well documented
resource to help us understand these critically timely issues

like few others could. Dr. Wallace does not stop there, but also looks beyond overused catchy headlines in order to "decode" the cleverly worded media rhetoric and uncover truths relating to the 'core' issues—both historically and legally—in a way that leads to practical as well as spiritual support of Israel. This is an approach that many who have wanted to do more for Israel in practical terms have been waiting for. This work is a spark of truth that will light a torch of justice.

—ROBERT STEARNS
PRESIDENT, EAGLES' WINGS

Dr. C.D. Wallace presents a crucial guidebook to the complicated issues of international law underlying Israel's sovereignty over the land of Israel and Jerusalem. This foundational book belongs in the arsenal of every advocate for truth and moral clarity in the Middle East.

—CALEV MYERS
FOUNDER AND CHIEF COUNSEL,
JERUSALEM INSTITUTE OF JUSTICE

There are few issues that are more neglected, misunderstood and misrepresented in the international debate arena than Israel's rights in the disputed territories. Whereas much attention has been given to the plight of the Palestinian people, little appears to be truly understood about Israel's rights to what are generally called the "occupied territories" but what really are "disputed territories."

Dr. Cynthia Wallace and the European Coalition for Israel have done a great service to those who are truly interested in the facts and not only fiction and myths, by presenting a clear legal perspective on this important issue. A final and comprehensive peace agreement in the Middle East can only be built upon historical facts and legal foundations. Through her well-researched and clearly presented document, Dr. Wallace has significantly contributed to a common understanding grounded in history and international law.

—AMBASSADOR DANNY AYALON
DEPUTY FOREIGN MINISTER
GOVERNMENT OF ISRAEL

FOUNDATIONS OF THE
INTERNATIONAL LEGAL RIGHTS
OF THE
JEWISH PEOPLE
and the
STATE OF ISRAEL
AND THE **IMPLICATIONS** FOR THE
PROPOSED NEW PALESTINIAN STATE

DR. CYNTHIA D. WALLACE

CREATION
HOUSE

FOUNDATIONS OF THE INTERNATIONAL LEGAL RIGHTS OF THE JEWISH PEOPLE AND THE STATE OF ISRAEL AND IMPLICATIONS FOR THE PROPOSED NEW PALESTINIAN STATE
By C.D. Wallace, PhD
Published by Creation House
A Charisma Media Company
600 Rinehart Road
Lake Mary, Florida 32746
www.charismamedia.com

Design Director: Bill Johnson
Cover design by Terry Clifton

Visit the author's website: DrCDWallace.com

Library of Congress Cataloging-in-Publication Data: 2011944545
International Standard Book Number: 978-1-61638-916-1
E-book International Standard Book Number: 978-1-61638-917-8

Photographs courtesy UNOG Library, League of Nations Archives

While the author has made every effort to provide accurate telephone numbers and Internet addresses at the time of publication, neither the publisher nor the author assumes any responsibility for errors or for changes that occur after publication.

First edition

12 13 14 15 16 — 987654321
Printed in Canada

TABLE OF CONTENTS

FOREWORD

A T A TIME when the legitimacy of the modern State of Israel is being increasingly challenged, it is of utmost importance to study not only the biblical but also the legal foundations of the Jewish State according to international law. Without a common understanding of the most central facts in the long and complex conflict in the Middle East, there can be no lasting peace. In order to become better informed we need to study the historical and legal evolution that has led to the reconstitution of the ancient Land of Israel.

Whereas most readers may well have a clear understanding of the biblical foundation for the Jewish State, many still lack a comprehensive historical and legal perspective. In order to present the legal instruments that form the basis for the modern State of Israel, Dr. Cynthia Day Wallace has engaged herself in writing the present book. With an impressive career in international law, in both academia and with the UN, spanning more than thirty years, she is highly qualified for this difficult but important task. Few scholars have managed to write not only with so much insight but also with such clarity, which will enable a broader audience get a better grasp of these issues.

This is a "must read" for anyone who wishes to defend the legal rights of the Jewish State. Although we can anticipate that the attacks on Israel will continue, we have no reason to give in or give up our defense. As Dr. Wallace documents in this book, the biblical narrative for Israel is substantially backed up by legally binding international agreements and historical facts and events. Reading this book will simply make you a more informed, better and more articulate friend of Israel.

—Tomas Sandell
Founding Director
European Coalition for Israel

European Coalition For Israel: A Call to Pray, Educate and Advocate

The European Coalition for Israel is a growing community of Christian individuals, associations and churches who wish to build better relations between Europe and Israel based on our common Judeo-Christian values. The organization was founded in 2003 and currently has offices in Brussels and Helsinki.

After having initially focused its activities only on the European Union, it has today a growing presence in the United Nations in Geneva and New York as well as in other international capitals around the world.

By combining a Biblical understanding of Israel with a legal and historical approach, it has been instrumental in helping many government leaders to understand the uniqueness of Israel and hence generate more political and spiritual support for the Jewish State.

A fifteen-minute video documentary on the message elaborated in the book is available at http://www.givepeaceachance.info.

You can find more information by visiting:
www.ec4i.org
or by e-mail at:
info@ec4i.org

INTRODUCTION

THERE IS PERHAPS no area in the world more sensitive or strategic to world security and peace than the Middle East, and arguably no country or city more central to this sensitivity than Israel and its capital and most Holy City Jerusalem.

There are as many opinions on the corresponding issues—even legally speaking—as there are proposed solutions. This is not only true of Israel itself and the territories it administers, but it extends to the city of Jerusalem and the many different views concerning its legal status.[1] Israel in general and Jerusalem in particular represent unique circumstances and, in many ways, do not fit into the normal legal parameters.

Taking Jerusalem, for example, there is no city anywhere that holds such deep-seated roots of religious and spiritual heritage and emotional and cultural bonds. These deep roots and the potential threats to their sanctity play an extraordinarily vital role in that city's significance and can seem to "trump" even national and international law norms in terms of relevance.

Why is this so vitally significant?

The Jewish heritage reaches back more than three thousand years, Jerusalem itself having been established perhaps more than 2,000 years before it was captured from the Jebusites by King David about 1,000 B.C. The Temple Mount in the Old City (in now so-called "East Jerusalem") is the site of the First and Second Jewish sacred Temples, containing the "Holy of Holies"—the most hallowed of all spiritual sites for the Jews. As regards the whole of the Land, expressed in their own words:

---

1   For "features" that may explain the reason for these many differences, and "why it is such a thorny problem in the peace process", see Ruth Lapidoth, "Jerusalem", in Rüdiger Wolfram, ed., *Max Planck Encyclopedia of Public International Law*, www.mpepil.com, at p. 1.

The Land of Israel was the birthplace of the Jewish people. Here their spiritual, religious and political identity was shaped.

After being forcibly exiled from their land, the people kept faith with it throughout their Dispersion (*Diaspora*) and never ceased to pray and hope for their return to it and for the restoration in it of their political freedom. Impelled by this historic and traditional attachment, Jews strove in every successive generation to re-establish themselves in their ancient homeland.[2]

Jerusalem is mentioned in the Bible by name more than six hundred times in the Old Testament alone, as well as throughout the New Testament, and has always been considered the "capital" for the Jewish people.

The Muslim connection dates back to the oral tradition of Mohammed's "miraculous night journey" ("*Miraj*"), in A.D. 621, on a "winged creature" from Mecca to the Temple Mount, accompanied by the Angel Gabriel, thus making it—with today's Al-Aqsa Mosque and Dome of the Rock—for many (though not all[3]) Muslims, the third holiest site of Islam, after Mecca and Medina. At the same time, even this "night ride", as referenced in verse 1 of Sura 17 of the Koran, does not mention Jerusalem at all, only "the farthest [*al-aqsa*] mosque". Since there was no mosque in Jerusalem at that time, the "farthest" mosque cannot have been the one now bearing that name on the Temple Mount in the Old City of ("East") Jerusalem. Still, Islamic tradition holds fast to this claim. In actual fact, early commentators interpreted the further place of worship as heaven. The city of Jerusalem is not once mentioned in the Koran, nor has Jerusalem ever served as the capital of Islam or of Arab-controlled Palestine,[4] under that or any other name.

The Christians date their heritage from the time of Christ, the

---

2   Declaration of the Establishment of the State of Israel, *Official Gazette:* No. 1, Tel Aviv, 5 Iyar 5708, 14.5.1948, at p. 1.

3   This does not apply to the Shia Muslims who number some 150 to 200 million people worldwide, since they revere Najaf, Karbalah, Qum, Isfahan, etc., well ahead of Jerusalem. (Appreciation to Salomon Benzimra, P.Eng., author of *The Jewish People's Rights to the Land of Israel,* Amazon Book, Kindle, 2011, for this observation, e-mail of 15 June 2011.)

4   Arab Palestinians held control over Jerusalem for only twenty-two years, from 1948–1967.

Jewish "Founder" of their faith, as well as reaching back to take in the entire history of the Jewish people, which was Christ's own heritage and which Christians regard as their own, mutually with the Jews. For Christians, the Holy Land is "holy" because that is where Jesus Christ was born, grew up, performed His ministry, was crucified, resurrected and ascended from the Mount of Olives, to which He promised to return.

But while the Christians are "at home" in every land in which they choose to dwell, and while the Arabs enjoy jurisdiction over vast areas of territory (twenty-one sovereign Arab States), the Jews have *only one* area of territorial "homeland": the small State of Israel. For the Jewish people, Israel is their *only* national home and Jerusalem their *only* Holy City and proclaimed "indivisible" capital. The very term *Wailing Wall*—as the Western Wall of the Temple was commonly called prior to the 1967 Jewish recapture of the Temple Mount, under Arab control since 1949—indicates the depth of the emotionally charged significance of this most sacred place for the Jewish people. As regards the whole of the Land, in the words of Dr. Chaim Weizmann (later president of the World Zionist Organization):

> As to the land that is to be the Jewish land there can be
> no question. Palestine alone, of all the countries in which
> the Jew has set foot throughout its long history, has an
> abiding place in his national tradition.[5]

The recognition of the Jewish people's singularly ancient *historic, religious, and cultural* link with an ancestral home has more *legal* significance than it may at first appear, and is easily bypassed in the current heated and polarized debate. These religious and spiritual claims are what have thus far made attempted solutions to territorial and other questions of international law in this area particularly delicate. The real issues are often lacking in clear definition and consensual interpretation of the relevant "law", at times even attributing to it a kind of *sui generis* (one of a kind, unique or "peculiar") character. International law, in itself, does not rely on religious or cultural ties but rather on accepted international law norms and standards, which is why the legal recognition of these *historical* aspects, in a *binding*

---

5   Chaim Weizmann, "Essay on Zionism", *reprinted in*: B. Litvinoff, ed., *The Letters and Papers of Chaim Weizmann*, University of Israel Press, Jerusalem, 1983 [hereinafter *Weizmann Papers*], Series B, Vol. I, Paper 28, pp. 134-142, at pp. 139-140.

international legal instrument, is so highly significant. It is precisely these *age-old historic ties* that remain *the most compelling reason for maintaining sovereignty over all the territory the Jewish people are legally entitled to under international law.*

The particular sacredness of this Land to such differing faiths is clearly demonstrated by the ongoing dispute over the governance of the Holy City of Jerusalem, from the Vatican to the United Nations, including periodic initiatives to give it a separate international legal status as a so-called *corpus separatum*. Indeed, because of the delicate and sensitive nature of these "spiritual" connections, Jerusalem is frequently left out altogether from discussions over other disputed territories such as the "West Bank"[6] and (earlier) Gaza.

The legal arguments will go on and on, with differing interpretations often even on the same side of the arguments. But the fundamental fact that the historical claims of the Zionist Organization, based on centuries-old connections between the Jewish people and "Palestine", were given recognition in a small town on the Italian Riviera named San Remo, in 1920, and confirmed unequivocally by the terms of the League of Nations Mandate for Palestine in 1922, takes on enormous significance when questions of territorial rights persist.

The ongoing and never-ending legal arguments and political posturing on both sides of the question of the "Palestine" statehood issue will not be resolved in these pages. Yet if the above basic truths with regard to ancestral territory are ignored, all the legal arguments in the world will not bring about an equitable solution. Thus it is important to see in what way(s) this most significant factor of historical ties has been endowed with a *legal* character and status that undergird Israel's legitimate rights in its Land as it confronts today's territorial conflicts.

While there is no way that the complex current political issues, a culmination of centuries of conflict and legal ambiguities, can be adequately dealt with in one brief exposé, one thing is certain: laws may change, perceptions may vary, but historical fact is immutable. Therefore, for the special case of Israel and Palestine, we need to look at fact rather than opinion and seek to avoid the promulgation of law that can result from persistent pressures of often misguided, misinformed and/or skillfully manipulated public opinion.

---

6   The designation "west bank" was first used by the Jordanians in 1950, after illegally (see Mandate for Palestine, Article 5) annexing the land, to differentiate it from the rest of the country on the east bank of the Jordan River.

Thus our mission here is not to attempt to pronounce legal judgments or to offer legal opinions, where even the best legal minds have not been able to achieve consensus, but rather to proclaim international legal truths in a largely political environment that is too frequently polluted with distortions of the truth and outright untruths.

A correlated intent here is to show where Israel's age-old historic links with the land intersect with legal parameters to give effect to its international legal status in the face of current political initiatives.

Accordingly it should be understood from the outset that the following is in no way intended to present itself as an exhaustive coverage of the many-faceted and age-long disputed issues relating to this territory. It is meant primarily as a wake-up call and/or reminder of the fundamental international legal rights of the Jewish people that were conferred beginning at the San Remo Conference in 1920 and that had threatened to all but slip into obscurity in the current debate, despite the fact that these rights have never been rescinded.

To accomplish these aims, we have only to revert back to the milestone international legal instrument, the Mandate for Palestine of 1922, which emerged from the 1920 San Remo sessions of the Paris Peace Conference of 1919 and in effect transformed the Balfour Declaration of 1917 (the "Magna Carta" of the Jewish people) into a legally binding international agreement that changed the course of history forever for the Jewish people worldwide.

Part I

FOUNDATIONS
OF THE
INTERNATIONAL LEGAL RIGHTS
OF THE JEWISH PEOPLE AND
THE STATE OF ISRAEL

BEFORE EXAMINING THE all-important international legal decisions made at San Remo in 1920, it is useful to trace back a few years to get a sense of the legal and political environment that followed in the wake of the dissolution of the Ottoman Empire in 1918, leading up to these significant legal and diplomatic events that both emerged from historical roots and went on to shape Jewish contemporary history.

1. THE BALFOUR DECLARATION

The history of the international legal turning point for the Jewish people begins in 1917. World War I was exposing a growing need of Jews dispersed all over the world to have a "national home", and in 1917 Prime Minister David Lloyd George expressed to the British War Cabinet that he "was convinced that a Jewish National Home was an historic necessity and that every opportunity should be granted to re-create a Jewish State".[7] This ultimately led to Great Britain issuing,

---

7   Abraham J. Edelheit, *History of Zionism—A Handbook and Dictionary* (Boulder, CO: Westview, 2000), at p. 309.

1

on 2 November 1917, a political declaration known as the "Balfour Declaration". This Declaration stated that:

His Majesty's Government view with favour the establishment in Palestine of a national home for the Jewish people, and will use their best endeavours to facilitate the achievement of this object, it being clearly understood that nothing should be done which may prejudice the civil and religious rights of existing non-Jewish communities in Palestine, or the rights and political status enjoyed by Jews in any other country.

As confirmed by Lord Balfour to Prime Minister Lloyd George:

Our justification for our policy is that we regard Palestine as being *absolutely exceptional*; that we consider the question of the Jews outside Palestine as one of world importance and that we conceive the Jews to have an historic claim to a home in *their ancient land*; provided that a home can be given them without either dispossessing or oppressing the present inhabitants... [emphasis added].[8]

This position was shared by the other Principal Allied and Associated Powers[9] who, in the words of Lord Balfour, "had committed themselves to the Zionist programme which inevitably excluded numerical self-determination".[10] Still, a *declaration* is not *law*, and a *British* declaration is not *international*. So while it is arguable that certain obligations of the Balfour Declaration were attributable to the British Government, it was *neither applicable to other States nor a binding instrument under international law.*

---

8   Pro. Fo. 371/4179.
9   See text accompanying notes 13 and 14, *infra*.
10   Pro. Fo. 800/217. See also *Documents on British Foreign Policy, 1919–1939*, E.L. Woodward and Rohan Butler, eds., Vol. IV, 1256–1278 (*reprinted in*: Walid Khalidi, ed., at pp. 195, 198).

2. Wilson's "Fourteen Points" and the League of Nations

At the time, the territory known as "Palestine" was still part of the Turkish Ottoman Empire, with which Britain and her allies were at war. Although the British forces entered Jerusalem in December 1917, the war with Turkey in Palestine continued into 1918. Once Britain liberated Palestine from Turkish rule in 1918, it was in a position to implement its policy.

Meanwhile, on 8 January 1918, U.S. President Woodrow ·Wilson delivered a speech to a joint session of the United States Congress that was to become known as his "Fourteen Points". Included in these points was the statement that the "Turkish portion of the present Ottoman Empire should be assured a secure sovereignty, but the other nationalities which are now under Turkish rule should be assured an undoubted security of life and an absolutely unmolested opportunity of autonomous development".[11] These Fourteen Points were accepted by some of the key Allied Powers and "informed" (influenced and were incorporated in part into) certain principles embodied in the Covenant of the League of Nations.

Thus the League of Nations was a direct result of the First World War, its Covenant or Articles of Organization being incorporated in the Treaty of Versailles, which entered into effect in January 1920.

3. San Remo Sessions of the Paris Peace Conference[12]

The next important milestone on the road to international legal status and a Jewish national home was the San Remo Conference, held at

---

11   Woodrow Wilson's Fourteen Points were first outlined in a speech he delivered to a joint session of the U.S. Congress on 8 January 1918. The quote is from Point 12.

12   The following sections on the San Remo Conference and its legacy borrow heavily upon—in some places recording verbatim or virtually verbatim (with the full agreement of the author)—Dr. Jacques Paul Gauthier's monumental work, *Sovereignty Over the Old City of Jerusalem: A Study of the Historical, Religious, Political and Legal Aspects of the Question of the Old City*, Thesis no. 725, University of Geneva, 2007. Part I of the present work draws liberally on Dr. Gauthier's thorough historical account. While some references to Gauthier's work are precisely cited, others are so interwoven, interchanged, interspersed and integrated with the author's own further research and formulations that it is virtually impossible to do proper justice to Dr. Gauthier in every

Villa Devachan in San Remo, Italy, from 18 to 26 April 1920. This was a post-World War I international reconvening of the Supreme Council of the Principal Allied Powers that had met together in Paris in 1919 with the powers of disposition over the territories which, as a consequence of World War I, had ceased to be under the sovereignty of the Ottoman Turkish Empire.

The Principal Allied Powers of World War I present at San Remo in 1920 were Great Britain, France, Italy and Japan. The United States had entered the war as an "Associated Power", rather than as a formal ally of France and Great Britain, in order to pursue its new policy of avoiding "foreign entanglements".[13] Thus while the United States was a member of the "Supreme Council of the Principal Allied and Associated Powers" of the Paris Peace Conference, and was known as one of the five "Great Powers", it is not to be associated with the term "Principal Allied Powers", of which there were four.[14] These four Powers were represented in San Remo by the Prime Ministers of Britain (David Lloyd George), France (Alexandre Millerand) and Italy (Francesco Nitti), and by Japan's Ambassador Keishiro Matsui. The United States was present as an "observer", represented by Robert Johnson, the U.S. Ambassador to Italy.

The San Remo Conference acted as an "extension" of the Paris Peace Conference, for the purpose of dealing with some outstanding issues that had not managed to be resolved in 1919, including certain claims and legal submissions made by key claimants in Paris, among which Zionist and Arab delegations. In San Remo, the aim of the Principal Allied Powers was to consider the claims, deliberate and hand down decisions on the legal recognition of each claim. The fundamental objective of the San Remo Conference, then, was effectively to decide the future of the Middle East following the collapse of the Ottoman Empire. In accordance with President Wilson's "Fourteen Points", it was not the intent of the victorious allies to acquire new colonies in the area but rather to establish there new sovereign States, over the course of time.

instance. His indulgence is gratefully acknowledged.
13   See Spencer C. Tucker, ed., *The European Powers in the First World War: An Encyclopedia* (New York: Garland, 1999), at pp. 1232, 1264.
14   Accordingly, it will be noted that the Paris Peace Treaties and other post-war peace settlements use the language: "Treaty of Peace between the *Allied and Associated* Powers and…[e.g. Germany or other treaty partner(s)]".

The Principal Allied Powers in San Remo were charged, *inter alia*, with responding to the claims that the Zionist Organization had submitted in February 1919 at the Peace Conference in Paris, while taking into consideration the submissions of the Arab delegation. (The Arab and Zionist delegations had pledged to support each other's claims.) The claims of the Zionist Organization included a demand for the recognition of "the historic title of the Jewish people to Palestine and the rights of the Jews to *reconstitute* their National Home in Palestine" (emphasis added).[15]

The boundaries of the "Palestine" referred to in these submissions included territories *west and east* of the Jordan River. The Zionist Organization had requested the appointment of Great Britain as Mandatory (or Trustee) of the League in respect of the Mandate over Palestine. The submissions specified that the ultimate purpose of the Mandate would be the "creation of an autonomous 'Commonwealth'", with the clear understanding "that nothing must be done that might prejudice the civil and religious rights of the non-Jewish communities at present established in Palestine, nor the rights and political status enjoyed by the Jews in all other countries".[16]

The policy to be given effect in the Mandate for Palestine was to be consistent with the Balfour Declaration in recognizing the historic, cultural and religious ties of the Jewish people to the Holy Land and the fundamental principle that Palestine should be the location of the re-established national home of the Jewish people. It is particularly relevant to underline the inclusion in the terms of the Mandate (through Article 2) of the fundamental principle set out in the Preamble of this international agreement that:

> recognition has thereby been given to the historical connection of the Jewish people with Palestine and to the grounds for *reconstituting* their national home in that country... [emphasis added].

Similarly consistent with the Balfour Declaration, as reiterated in the submissions to the Paris Peace Conference, the Mandate's Preamble retained the condition that: "nothing shall be done which may prejudice the civil and religious rights of existing non-Jewish

15   Opening submission of the Zionist Organization, point (1), *reprinted in*: *Weizmann Papers*, *supra* note 5, Paper 51, pp. 221–232, at p. 223.
16   *Ibid*, point (4).

communities in Palestine, or the rights and political status enjoyed by Jews in any other country". This conferred no *new* rights on either the non-Jewish inhabitants of Palestine or the Jewish populations in other countries; it merely preserved existing rights in both cases (see also Articles 2, 6, 9, and 13). The Mandate can nonetheless be regarded as affecting the Jewish people worldwide to the extent that it provided a national home for all Jews everywhere to return to, encouraging settlement in Palestine and therefore immigration (Article 6) and facilitating the acquisition of citizenship (Article 7). It was anticipated that non-Jews would live as a protected population within the Jewish national home.

4. THE DECISION OF THE PRINCIPAL ALLIED POWERS RELATING TO THE MANDATE FOR PALESTINE

The Allied Powers, assembled in San Remo to deliberate this and other submissions, recognized that not all areas of the Middle East were yet ready for full independence. So they agreed to set up Mandates for each territory, with one of the Allied Powers to be in charge of implementing each Mandate, respectively, "until such time as [the territories] are able to stand alone".[17]

Initially three Mandates were assigned—one over both Syria and Lebanon, one over Mesopotamia (Iraq) and one over Palestine. In the first two Mandates, the native inhabitants were recognized as having the capacity to govern themselves, with the Mandatory Power merely serving to advise and facilitate the establishment of the necessary institutions of government. Accordingly, Article 1 of the Mandate for Mesopotamia states:

> The Mandatory will frame within the shortest possible time, not exceeding three years from the date of the coming into force of this Mandate, an Organic Law for Mesopotamia. This Organic Law shall be framed *in consultation with the native authorities,* and shall take account of the rights, interests and wishes of *all the populations inhabiting the mandated territory* [emphasis added].

---

17   See San Remo Resolution, Appendix III, para. (c).

The language notably differed in the case of the Mandate for Palestine, in which it was specifically stipulated in Article 4 that:

> An appropriate *Jewish agency* shall be recognised as a public body for the purpose of advising and co-operating with the Administration of Palestine: in such economic, social and other matters as may affect the establishment of the *Jewish national home and the interests of the Jewish population in Palestine*, and, subject always to the control of the Administration, to assist and take part in "the development of the country". *The Zionist organisation*, so long as its organisation and constitution are in the opinion of the Mandatory appropriate, shall be recognised as such agency [emphasis added].

So while the Preamble states that it is "clearly understood that nothing should be done which might prejudice the *civil* and *religious* rights of existing *non*-Jewish communities in Palestine", the *political* authority was explicitly vested in the *Jewish people,* with the ultimate objective of the establishment of the *Jewish national home.* The language of the Mandate persistently refers specifically to the reconstituted *"national home"* for the Jewish people. Although the Jewish people were part of the indigenous population of Palestine, the majority of them at that time were not living in the Land. At the same time, while the civil and religious rights of the Arab and other inhabitants were safeguarded, including voting rights, no sovereign political rights were assigned to them. (It is of significance that the Mandate did not distinguish these non-Jewish inhabitants similarly as "a people" or as lacking a "national home".)

Thus the Mandate for Palestine differed significantly from those established for the other former Ottoman Asiatic territories, setting out *how the Land was to be settled by the Jewish people* in preparation for their forming a viable nation within the territory then known as "Palestine".[18] The *unique* obligations of the Mandatory to the Jewish people in respect of the establishment of their national home

---

18   It should be noted that the geographical area of Palestine was not identical to that which pertained when it was part of the Ottoman Empire, the borders being left undefined.

in Palestine thus gave a *sui generis* (one of a kind, unique) character to the Mandate for Palestine.

It is also important to note that, pursuant to Article 5 of the Mandate:

> [N]*o Palestine territory shall be ceded or leased to, or in any way placed under the control of the government of any foreign Power* [emphasis added].

So having considered the claims, deliberated and reached a decision, the parties to the San Remo Conference produced *binding resolutions* relating to the recognition of claims to the Ottoman territories presented in Paris. These members of the Supreme Council thus reached an agreement that had the force of a *legally binding decision* of the Powers with the right to dispose of the territories in question.

Accordingly, the Principal Allied Powers, in conformity with the provisions of Article 22 of the Covenant of the League of Nations, decided to entrust to Great Britain the Mandate for Palestine which involved a "sacred trust of civilization" in respect of "the establishment in Palestine of a national home for the Jewish people",[19] thus confirming the decision made a few months earlier by these same Powers at a conference in London in February of that year.

The decision made in San Remo was a watershed moment in the history of the Jewish people, who had been a people without a home for some two thousand years. From the perspective of Dr. Chaim Weizmann, president of the newly formed Zionist Organization and later to become the first President of the State of Israel, the decision made relating to the destiny of Palestine at the San Remo sessions of the Paris Peace Conference was a turning point in the history of the Jewish people. In Weizmann's own words:

> [R]ecognition of our rights in Palestine is embodied in the treaty with Turkey,[[20]] and has become part of international law. This is the most momentous political event in the whole history of our movement, and it is, perhaps,

19   Minutes of Meeting of the Supreme Council of the Allied Powers in San Remo at the Villa Devachan—25 April 1920 (under "It was agreed-... (b) That the terms of the mandates article should be as follows:").
20   The reference here is to the Treaty of Sèvres (see note 27, *infra*).

no exaggeration to say in the whole history of our people since the Exile. For this great declaration of deliverance we have to thank the Allied and Associated Powers...[21]

To the Zionist Organization of America, the decision of the Supreme Council of the Principal Allied Powers "crown[ed] the British declaration[22] by enacting it as part of the law of nations of the world".[23]

There are a number of points that should be noted concerning the San Remo decision.[24]

1. For the first time in history, Palestine became a legal entity. Hitherto it had been just a geographical area.

2. All relevant agreements prior to the San Remo Conference were superseded. (Although not all specifically named at the Conference, this would include both the Sykes-Picot agreement[25] and the Feisal-Weizmann agreement.[26])

3. The Balfour Declaration, which had been given recognition by many Powers prior to San Remo, achieved international legal status.

---

21   From Weizmann's speech to the annual Zionist conference of July 1920, *reprinted in*: *Weizmann Papers, supra* note 5, Paper 58, pp. 290-296, at p. 290.

22   The reference here is to the Balfour Declaration (see Appendix I, *infra*).

23   Statement of the Zionist Organization of America, PRO.FO, 371/5114.

24   These points are derived from a lecture by Howard Grief in San Remo on 24 April 2010, as noted by Roy Thurley, "90 Years On: Legal Aspects of Jewish Rights in the Mandate for Palestine", CFI Communications, Eastbourne UK, 2010, at pp. 4–5.

25   The Sykes–Picot Agreement of 1916 (in official terminology, "the 1916 Asia Minor Agreement") was a secret agreement reached during World War I between the British and French Governments, with the assent of imperial Russia, defining their respective spheres of influence and control in Western Asia after the expected downfall of the Ottoman Empire during World War I.

26   The Feisal-Weizmann Agreement of 1919, signed by Emir Feisal (son of the King of Hejaz) and Chaim Weizmann (later president of the World Zionist Organization) was part of the Paris Peace Conference of 1919, settling disputes stemming from World War I. It is noteworthy that, although it was short-lived, the agreement was for Arab-Jewish cooperation on the development of a *Jewish homeland in Palestine and an Arab nation in a large part of the Middle East, not in Palestine.*

4. "Jewish people" were designated as beneficiaries of a sacred trust in the Mandate, the first step on the road leading to national sovereignty, even though most of the Jews had not yet returned to their Land.

5. Henceforward, transfer of the title on Palestine could not be revoked, either by the League of Nations or the United Nations as its successor, unless the Jewish people should choose to give up their title.

6. The San Remo decisions were incorporated into the Treaty of Sèvres,[27] signed on 10 August 1920 by, *inter alia*, the four Principal Powers and Turkey. [Note: Although the treaty was never ratified by Turkey,[28] the same parties (including Turkey) did sign and ratify the superseding Treaty of Lausanne in 1923.[29]]

7. The Arabs gained even greater rights in Lebanon, Syria and Mesopotamia, as they were considered ready, or near ready, for autonomy.

8. The San Remo decision marks the end of the longest colonized period in history, lasting around 1,800 years.

With reference to the historic connection of the Jews with Palestine, as recognized in the Mandate, Churchill wrote in his White Paper of 1922, shortly before the Mandate's adoption by the League of Nations:

… it is essential that [the Jewish community in Palestine] should know that it is in Palestine as of right and not on sufferance. That is the reason why it is necessary that the existence of a Jewish National Home in Palestine should be internationally guaranteed, and that it should be formally recognized to rest upon ancient historic connection.[30]

---

27   The Treaty of Peace Between the Allied and Associated Powers and Turkey, signed at Sèvres, 10 August 1920, *The Treaties of Peace 1919–1923, Vol. II,* Carnegie Endowment for International Peace, New York, 1924.

28   The Treaty of Sèvres was annulled in the course of the Turkish War of Independence.

29   See Part I, section 9, *infra.*

30   The Churchill White Paper of 1922, London: HMSO, Cmd 1700, "British Policy in Palestine", published June 1922, *reprinted in: Weizmann Papers, supra* note 5, Paper 80, pp.

5. The League of Nations and the Mandate for Palestine

The ultimate Mandate for Palestine approved by the Council of the League of Nations on 24 July 1922 explicitly refers back to the decisions of the Supreme Council of the Principal Allied Powers of 25 April 1920. The Mandate begins: "Whereas the Principal Allied Powers have agreed...". Upon approval by the League Council, the Mandate became binding on all fifty-one members of the League. Since the United States officially endorsed the terms of the Mandate but had not joined the League of Nations, special negotiations between Great Britain and the United States with regard to the Palestine Mandate had been successfully concluded in May 1922 and approved by the Council of the League in July. The United States ultimately signed a bilateral treaty with Britain (on 3 December 1924),[31] actually incorporating the text of the Mandate for Palestine, thus completing its legal alignment with the terms of the Mandate under the League of Nations.

This act of the League Council enabled the ultimate realization of "the long cherished dream of the *restoration* of the Jewish people to *their ancient land*" and validated "*the existence of historical facts and events linking the Jewish people to Palestine*. For the members of the Supreme Council, these *historical facts* were considered to be *accepted and established*" (emphasis added).[32] In the words of Neville Barbour, "*In 1922, international sanction was given to the Balfour Declaration by the issue of the Palestine Mandate*".[33]

In actual fact, the Mandate went *beyond* the Balfour Declaration of 1917. The incorporation, in the Preamble of the Mandate, of the principle that Palestine should be *reconstituted* as the national home of the Jewish people represented a deliberate broadening of the policies contained in the Balfour Declaration, which did not explicitly include the concept of *reconstitution*. It is of some interest that, while the word "reconstitute" was absent from the Balfour Declaration, it was actually Lord Balfour himself who ensured the inclusion of this concept in the final, legally binding Mandate.

415–420, at p. 417.

31   The Anglo American Treaty of 1924, 44 Stat. 2184; Treaty Series 728.

32   Gauthier, *supra* note 12, at p. 824; see also *ibid.*, Chapter IV, Section III.5.

33   Neville Barbour, *Nisi Dominus— A Survey of the Palestine Controversy* (London: George G. Harrap, 1946), at p. 5.

Thus it was not a new idea, "grafted on" at the last moment, but was well deliberated. The ultimate effect was that the rights of the Jewish people under the Mandate for Palestine were thereby *greater* than the rights contemplated in its source document, the Balfour Declaration. According to Abraham Baumkoller:

> [T]he choice of the term *"reconstitute"* clearly indicates that in the eyes of the Council, it was not a question of creating something new, but of admitting the *reconstitution* of a situation that already existed ages ago. This idea coincides, if you will, with the notion of "historic ties", even if these are not altogether identical [emphasis added].[34]

In addition to the insertion of the *"reconstituting"* language, the phrase in the Mandate's Article 2: "...*will secure* the establishment" (of the Jewish national home, as laid down in the Preamble of the Mandate) could equally be said to go beyond the Balfour Declaration which uses the considerably milder language: "...*view with favour* the establishment in Palestine of a national home for the Jewish people" and *"will use their best endeavours to facilitate* the achievement of this object".

Looking beyond the details, the important point is that the *primary objective of the Mandate* to provide *a national home for the Jewish people*—including Jewish people dispersed *worldwide*—in their ancestral Land, had been fulfilled. The Arab people, who already exercised jurisdictional sovereignty in a large number of States,[35] were guaranteed protection of their civil and religious rights under the Mandate as long as they wished to remain—even after the State of Israel was ultimately formed in 1948—including citizenship if they so chose. Moreover, for the Arab population, Trans-Jordan had meanwhile been added as a territory under Arab sovereignty, *carved out of Palestine itself, the very mandated territory at issue*, prior to the actual signing of the Mandate in 1922 under the League of Nations.

In sum, the Mandate for Palestine, approved by the Council of the League of Nations in July 1922, was an international treaty and, as such, was legally binding. The International Court of Justice (I.C.J.) has since confirmed that the Mandate instrument "in fact and in

34   Abraham Baumkoller, *Le mandat sur la Palestine* (Paris: Rousseau, 1931), at p. 150 [translated into English from the original French by the present author].
35   The Arab people have twenty-one sovereign States.

law, is an international agreement having the character of a treaty or convention".[36]

6. THE MANDATE FOR PALESTINE AS IT PERTAINS TO JERUSALEM AND THE OLD CITY

The rights granted to the Jewish people in the Mandate for Palestine relating to the establishment of the Jewish national home were to be given effect in all parts and regions of the Palestine territory. No exception was made for Jerusalem and its Old City, which were not singled out for special reference in either the Balfour Declaration or the Mandate for Palestine, other than to call for the preservation of existing rights in the Holy Places. As concerns the Holy Places, including those located in the Old City, specific obligations and responsibilities were imposed on the Mandatory.

It follows that the *legal rights* of the claimants to sovereignty over the *Old City of Jerusalem* similarly derive from the decisions of the Principal Allied Powers in San Remo and from the terms of the Mandate for Palestine approved by the Council of the League of Nations. In evaluating the validity of the claims of Israel relating to the Old City, the Council decision is of great significance from the perspective of the rights and obligations that it created under international law. In the view of Oxford international law professor Ian Brownlie, "in many instances the rights of parties to a dispute derive from legally significant acts, or a treaty concluded very long ago".[37] As a result of these "legally significant acts", there are *legal* as well as *historical* ties between the State of Israel and the Old City.

The *intellectual* ties were further solidified by the official opening of the Hebrew University on 1 April 1925 in Jerusalem, attended by many dignitaries, including the University's founding father, Dr. Chaim Weizmann, Field Marshall Allenby, Lord Balfour, Professor William Rappard and Sir Herbert Samuel, among many other distinguished guests. According to Dr. Weizmann, addressing the dignitaries and some twelve thousand other attendees at this memorable event, the opening of the University in Jerusalem was "the distinctive

---

36 See International Court of Justice, *South West Africa Cases (Preliminary Objections)*, *I.C.J. Reports* (1962), at pp. 319, 330–332.
37 Ian Brownlie, *Principles of Public International Law*, 5th ed (Oxford: Clarendon Press, 1998), at p. 129.

symbol, as it is destined to be the crowning glory, of the National Home which we are seeking to rebuild"[38]

In addition to the *legal, historical* and *intellectual* heritage, in the words of Jerusalem scholar Dr. Jacques Paul Gauthier: "To attempt to solve the Jerusalem / Old City problem without taking into consideration the historical and *religious* facts is like trying to put together a ten thousand piece puzzle without the most strategic pieces of that puzzle"[39] In his monumental work entitled *Sovereignty Over the Old City of Jerusalem: A Study of the Historical, Religious, Political and Legal Aspects of the Question of the Old City,*[40] Dr. Gauthier offers an exhaustive review of these historical/spiritual/political/legal bonds,[41] emphasizing the "extraordinary meaning" of the Old City of Jerusalem and the temple to the Jewish people.[42]

Indeed, with respect to the question of the Old City, the historical facts and the *res religiosae* (or things involving religion) are rendered legally relevant by the decisions taken at the San Remo sessions of the Paris Peace Conference, together with the terms of the Mandate for Palestine. Notwithstanding the fact that historical, religious or other non-legal considerations may not be considered relevant or sufficient to support a legal claim normally in international law cases, these aspects of the issue of the city of Jerusalem are relevant in evaluating the claims of Israel and the Palestinians relating to sovereignty over the Old City, just as much or perhaps even more than over the entire State of Israel and the Holy Land, as noted in the Introduction.

7. Arab Opposition

The Arabs of Palestine did not want to give up *any* of the land and, among other objections, generally took the position that the terms of the Mandate for Palestine relating to the establishment of a Jewish national home there contravened the provisions of Article 22 of the Covenant of the League of Nations (setting up the Mandates). This argument is, however, not valid regarding the Mandate for Palestine, since the Principal Allied Powers who were the founders of the League of Nations and the authors of its Covenant had specifically approved the inclusion of the policies of the Balfour Declaration in

---

38   *Reprinted in: Weizmann Papers, supra* note 5, Paper 87, pp. 442-445, at p. 445.
39   Gauthier, *supra* note 12, at p. 806.
40   See *ibid.*
41   See *ibid.,* Chapter II, Section II, at p. 812.
42   See *ibid.,* Chapter II, Section I.

the Mandate for Palestine in San Remo in April 1920. The members of the League of Nations did not challenge the validity of this Mandate after it was approved by the Council of the League in July 1922. The Council was very much aware of the objections of the Arabs of Palestine when it decided to approve the terms of the Mandate.

8. THE 1921 PARTITION OF PALESTINE

One possible exception regarding the Mandatory's obligations was that relating to the "territories lying between the Jordan and the eastern boundary of Palestine" (Article 25). In March 1921, in Cairo, Great Britain decided to partition the mandated territory of Palestine, for international political reasons of its own.[43] Article 25 of the Mandate gave the Mandatory Power permission to "postpone or withhold" most of the terms of the Mandate in the area of land east of the Jordan River ("Trans-Jordan"), if it did not consider them to be applicable. Great Britain, as Mandatory Power, exercised that right.

The Palestine partition proposal was approved by the Council of the League of Nations on 16 September 1922. Thus from 1921–1922 there was not yet any effective "partition", only a separate administration. The Zionist Organization presented its objections to this partition decision because part of the "Promised Land" was located on the east bank of the Jordan River (referred to in Hebrew as *Everhayarden*). Therefore,

> ...to all intents and purposes [*Trans-Jordan was*] *an integral part of Palestine.* We do not differentiate in our sentimental and historical relation between west and east of the Jordan [emphasis added].[44]

Sir Hersch Lauterpacht—one-time Cambridge international law professor and *ad hoc* judge at the International Court of Justice, and considered one of the leading international lawyers of the twentieth century—expressed the opinion that this fundamental modification of the Mandate for Palestine made by Great Britain and later approved by the Council of the League of Nations contravened the terms of the

---

43 See text accompanying note 48, *infra*. See also Gilbert, *Churchill and the Jews*, *infra* note 48, at pp. 47-51.

44 From address by Chaim Weizmann of 21 November 1926 in Boston, *reprinted in*: *Weizmann Papers, supra* note 5, Paper 95, pp. 484–498, at p. 491, as quoted by Gauthier, *infra* note 12, Chapter V, Section II.2.

Mandate for Palestine, which was an *international treaty* concluded between the Principal Allied Powers and the Mandatory Power. For Lauterpacht, the consent of the Principal Allied Powers should have been obtained prior to modifying one of the material terms of the Mandate agreement. Furthermore, the modification failed to protect the rights of *non-Arabs* in Trans-Jordan, in marked contrast to the protection of the rights of *non-Jews* in the rest of (Jewish) Palestine (later, Israel).

In actual fact, the language of Article 25 ("postpone or withhold") suggests that this provision was meant to be temporary. Whatever the case, once the territory of Palestine was partitioned, Winston Churchill—British Colonial Secretary at the time—reaffirmed the commitment of Great Britain to give effect to the policies of the Balfour Declaration in *all the other parts of the territory* covered by the Mandate for Palestine west of the Jordan River. *This pledge included the area of Jerusalem and its Old City.* In Churchill's own words:

> It is manifestly right that the Jews who are scattered all over the world should have a national centre and a national home where some of them may be reunited. And where else could that be but in the land of Palestine, with which for more than 3000 years they have been intimately and profoundly associated?[45]

The effect of the partition of the territory covered by the Palestine Mandate was that 90,000 square kilometers out of a total area of about 117,000 square kilometers—representing about 78 percent of the territory under the Mandate granted to Great Britain in Palestine—was placed under partial control of an Arab government.

The increasing tensions during the next decades between Jews and Arabs in the remnant of the territory covered by the Mandate was, according to Chaim Weizmann, partially attributable to the fact that:

> ...in the dead of the night Trans-Jordan had been separated from Palestine. *When the policy of the National Home was framed, eastern and western Palestine were considered a unit.* Suddenly, more than half [in fact

---

45   PRO. CO. 733/2.

over *three quarters of*] the territory was cut off and an embargo laid on it as far as Jewish colonization was concerned [emphasis added].[46]

There was no new Mandate for Trans-Jordan. It was still covered by the Mandate for Palestine. Thus Great Britain continued as the Mandatory Power over both Jewish and Arab portions. The real partition was finally consummated only in 1946 when, on 25 May, Trans-Jordan achieved independence, relying on the support of Great Britain and the endorsement of the Council of the League of Nations. For former Israeli Ambassador to the UN, Professor Yehuda Zvi Blum, *the rights vested in the Arab people of Palestine with respect to the principle of self-determination were fulfilled as a result of this initial partition of Palestine approved by the Council of the League of Nations in 1922.* According to Professor Blum:

> *The Palestinian Arabs have long enjoyed self-determination in their own state – the Palestinian Arab State of Jordan* [emphasis added].[47]

Worth mentioning here, Colonel T.E. Lawrence ("Lawrence of Arabia"), in a letter apparently written on 17 January 1921, informed Churchill's private secretary that he had reached an "agreement" with Emir Feisal, the eldest son of King Hussein (internationally recognized King of Hejaz and self-proclaimed King of all Arabs). Feisal—a man said by Lawrence to be known for keeping his word—had agreed that in return for Arab sovereignty in Iraq, Trans-Jordan and Syria, he would *abandon all claims of his father to Palestine.*[48] While such

---

46   *Reprinted in: Weizmann Papers, supra* note 5, Paper 116, pp. 590–593, at p. 591.

47   On behalf of Israel, in submissions to the UN General Assembly on 2 December 1980, United Nations General Assembly Official Records (GAOR), XXXVth Session, Plenary Meetings, 77th Meeting, 1318, para. 108.

48   See Sir Martin Gilbert, *Churchill and the Jews,* Simon and Schuster, 2007, at pp. 45–46. This 'agreement' should be taken into account when objections arise that pledges made in 1915 through the so-called "McMahon-Hussein Correspondence" with regard to support by the British for independence of the Arabs in return for Arab support of the British against the Turks in World War I were not kept. Although the British position that the area of Palestine was never included is disputed by the Arabs, the Arabs of that particular region did *not* in fact rise up in support of the British against the Ottoman Turks and thus did not in any case fulfil the conditions. In any event, all formal and informal agreements were ultimately superseded when territorial arrangements initiated by the Balfour Declaration were raised to the level of a legally binding instrument by the League of Nations in the Mandate for Palestine.

an agreement cannot be enforced under international law, Great Britain would seem to have accepted this condition in good faith and acted upon it in a way that had *legally binding consequences.* As recently as 1981, King Hussein of Jordan himself exclaimed: *"The truth is that Jordan is Palestine and Palestine is Jordan".*[49]

This is apart from the fact that, before the dissolution of the League of Nations on 17 April 1946, all the so-called *Class A* mandates (i.e. those mandated territories that had been deemed ready or near ready for self-government), including the Hashemite[50] Kingdom of Trans-Jordan, had become autonomous or gained their independence—all *except* for the territory covered by the Mandate for Palestine located west of the Jordan River. It should be remarked that the partition of Palestine by Great Britain did not remove the rights under the terms of the Mandate for Palestine of the Arab inhabitants of the territory of Palestine located west of the Jordan River.

History is left to judge how Britain carried out the "sacred trust" vested in her by the League of Nations.

9. The Treaty of Lausanne

One year after the approval of the Mandate for Palestine by the Council of the League of Nations, on 24 July 1923, the Treaty of Lausanne[51] was signed by Turkey. While this Treaty contained no specific reference to Palestine, by its Article 16 Turkey renounced "all rights and title whatsoever over or respecting the territories" which implicitly included Palestine, "the future of these territories and islands being settled or to be settled by the parties concerned". Turkey thereby relinquished all rights and title over the region (including

---

49   King Hussein, 1981. Further similar statements: "We are the government of Palestine, the army of Palestine and the refugees of Palestine". Prime Minister of Jordan,
Hazza' al-Majali, 23 August 1959. "Palestine and Transjordan are one". King Abdullah,
Arab League meeting in Cairo, 12 April 1948. "Palestine is Jordan and Jordan is Palestine; there is one people and one land, with one history and one and the same fate".
Prince Hassan, brother of King Hussein, addressing the Jordanian National Assembly,
2 February 1970. "Jordan is not just another Arab state with regard to Palestine, but
rather, Jordan is Palestine and Palestine is Jordan in terms of territory, national
identity, sufferings, hopes and aspirations". Jordanian Minister of Agriculture, 24 September 1980, quotes assembled by Melanie Phillips, "Jordan is Palestine", *The Spectator,*
21 June 2010, http://www.spectator.co.uk/melaniephillips/6094074/jordan-is-palestine.
thtml.
50   The Hashemites were the most powerful Arab tribe of that time.
51   Treaty of Peace with Turkey Signed at Lausanne, 24 July 1923, *The Treaties of Peace
1919-1923, Vol. II,* New York: Carnegie Endowment for International Peace, 1924.

Jerusalem and its Old City). This paved the way for the entry into force of the Mandate for Palestine on 29 September 1923, when the British officially assumed control of the Palestine Mandate.[52]

10. The UN Partition Plan—Resolution 181 (II) and Arab Rejection

After the Second World War, the League of Nations was disbanded and a new international peacekeeping body, the United Nations Organization, was set up. This new body inherited all the agreements made by its predecessor, including the Mandate for Palestine. In 1947 Britain decided to terminate her stewardship of the Mandate and notified the United Nations accordingly. It should be noted that *the Mandate itself was not terminated* but only Britain's stewardship of it. In a similar way, Britain's stewardship of the Trans-Jordan portion of the Mandate had been terminated the previous year by virtue of that territory gaining its independence.

In November 1947, the United Nations proposed a Partition Plan for Palestine (Resolution 181 (II)), recommending the setting up— in the remaining 22 percent of the original Palestinian Mandate— of another Arab State, a Jewish State and an international zone to include Jerusalem. This Resolution to consider partition, as is the case with all UN General Assembly Resolutions, was only a *recommendation*.[53] It was accepted by the Jewish leadership but rejected by the Arabs. This important fact is often left out of the debate. It should also be noted that if UN Resolution 181 were valid today (which it is not), then so would be the provision in Part III-D that stipulates that after ten years, Jerusalem's international status could be subject to a

---

52   See League of Nations Official Journal, November 1923, 4th Year, No. 11, Twenty-Sixth Session of the Council, paras. 1087 and 1092, at pp. 1349, 1355.

53   Security Council Resolutions are legally binding only where international peace and security are threatened, as specified in Chapter VII of the Charter ("Action with Respect to Threats to the Peace, Breaches of the Peace, and Acts of Aggression"). Resolutions made under Chapter VI ("Pacific Settlement of Disputes") are *not* legally binding, primarily because there is no international enforcement mechanism. (See e.g. Hillier, Timothy, Taylor & Francis Group. *Sourcebook on Public International Law,* London: Cavendish Publishing, 1998, at p. 568; Philippe Sands, Pierre Klein, D. W. Bowett, *Bowett's Law of International Institutions,* London: Sweet & Maxwell, 2001, at p. 46; *et alia.*) Exceptions are made by certain States that give constitutional or special legal status to the UN Charter and Security Council resolutions. (See generally, e.g., *National Implementation of United Nations Sanctions: A Comparative Study,* Vera Gowlland-Debbas, Djacoba Liva Tehindrazanarivelo, The Hague: Brill, 2004; John Dugard, *Recognition and the United Nations,* Cambridge UK: Cambridge University Press, 1987.)

referendum of all Jerusalem residents as to a change in the status of
the city—a decision that today, as in the past, would have been made
by Jerusalem's decisive Jewish majority.

Around the time of the reconstitution of Israel as a State, in May
1948, there was some talk of reviving the Partition Plan, but by the
end of Israel's forced 1948 War of Independence and the conclusion
of the 1949 armistice agreements, Resolution 181 had become largely
moot, as the establishment meanwhile of a military armistice-line
(the "Green line") had created the expectation of an ensuing negotiation of peace treaties.

A July 1949 working paper of the UN Secretariat entitled "The
Future of Arab Palestine and the Question of Partition" noted further that:

> The Arabs rejected the United Nations Partition Plan so
> that any comments of theirs did not specifically concern
> the status of the Arab section of Palestine under partition
> but rather rejected the scheme in its entirety.[54]

Israel was ready to declare its independence when it felt it was able
to meet all the criteria and international prerequisites of statehood
and assume full international legal responsibility. The actual declaration of statehood was somewhat hastened by the earlier than anticipated withdrawal of British forces, resulting in the State of Israel
being born at midnight on 14 May 1948.[55] This event basically fulfilled the ultimate aim of the drafters of the San Remo decision nearly
thirty years before.

While the primary objective of the Mandate for Palestine had
been achieved, the State established in 1948 was not exactly what was
contemplated in San Remo in 1920, where the Jewish national home
was first envisaged as including Palestinian territory on both sides of
the Jordan (as was the case in *Eretz Yisrael*). In any case, Israel's new
status as a nation-state, essentially west of the Jordan River, was effectively confirmed and "officially" recognized by the United Nations

---

54   UN document A/AC.25/W.19.
55   The British had notified the UN of their intent to terminate the Mandate for the
remaining part of Palestine (outside of Trans-Jordan) no later than 1 August 1948. Then
early in 1948, they announced their resolve to end the Mandate on 14 May. The Jewish
leadership, under future Prime Minister David Ben-Gurion, accordingly declared independence on the afternoon of Friday, 14 May 1948, with the declaration to become
effective from the end of the Mandate at midnight of that day.

upon its acceptance of Israel into membership on 11 May 1949, one year after Britain's termination of the Mandate and Israel's simultaneous declaration of independence. Thus, Israel's statehood does *not* rely, as many suppose, on the United Nations Partition Plan of 1947 (Resolution 181). In a word, *the primary foundations in international law for the "legal" claim based on "historic rights" or "historic title" of the Jewish people in respect of Palestine are the San Remo decisions of April 1920, the Mandate for Palestine of July 1922 and the Covenant of the League of Nations (Article 22).* These instruments alone constitute the "Charter of Freedom" of the Jewish people.

Part II

THE QUESTION
OF A
UNILATERAL DECLARATION
OF A PALESTINIAN STATE

In order to get the proper perspective in considering the international legal framework surrounding the question of a unilaterally declared Palestinian State with the Old City of Jerusalem as its capital, we need first to go to some of the sources of contention. As this involves making reference to highly controversial "core" issues, the main aim here is *not* to presume to cover all aspects of each issue and/or offer cursory or facile legal opinions. Indeed, as mentioned at the outset—and, if anything, far more applicable here—it should be emphasized that the following is in no way intended to be anything like an exhaustive coverage of the many-faceted and age-long disputed issues relating to this contested territory. The objective is rather to provoke some new thinking beyond the current clichés and to raise awareness over ('innocent' or intentional) (mis)usages of language to influence and manipulate public opinion and potentially culminate in ill-founded legally binding decisions with long-term consequences.

As in Part I, in order to gain a better understanding of the roots of the current heated debate, a brief look at the historical setting out of which today's issues arise is needed. This will help to make sense out of the following efforts at connecting the historical legal foundations with the current debate.

1. Israel's War of Independence

On 15 May 1948, one day after the creation of the State of Israel, the new Jewish State was invaded by five Arab armies (Egypt, Syria, Jordan, Iraq and Lebanon), afterward reinforced by other Arab forces. By the time hostilities ceased in January 1949, Israel had lost a significant part of its mandated territory to the invading forces—namely, Judea and Samaria (including the eastern part of Jerusalem) to Trans-Jordan, and the Gaza Strip to Egypt. Such an invasion, unilaterally or collectively, for the purpose of acquiring territory, is contrary to international law. Whereas Egypt only *occupied* its captured territory, Trans-Jordan illegally *annexed* Judea and Samaria and called the combined entity the "west bank" in order to link the territory with the east bank of the Jordan. This annexation was only recognized by two nations, namely, Britain and Pakistan. It should be noted that, in any case, recognition of annexation, however limited or general, has no bearing upon the question of legality under international law.

The areas captured by the surrounding Arab countries by the time of the 1949 Armistice Agreements continued under Arab control until the Six-Day War of June 1967.

2. The Six-Day War

The Six-Day War, fought from 5 to 10 June 1967 between Israel on the one hand and Egypt, Jordan and Syria on the other, was a swift and decisive victory for Israel, allowing it to reclaim those territories it had lost in 1948. From Israel's perspective, this was a defensive war, since, for example, on 15 May, Israel's Independence Day, Egyptian troops had begun moving into the Sinai and massing near the Israeli border, and by 18 May, Syrian troops as well were positioned for battle along the Golan Heights. Egypt had also paved the way for war by ordering the removal of special UN peacekeeping forces in the Sinai as of 16 May, a withdrawal that, absent any consultation with the UN General Assembly, was completed within three days.[56] Then on 22 May, Egypt had effectively declared war by blocking the Straits of Tiran in the Gulf of Aqaba, Israel's vital trading and supply link to the rest of the world; and by 31 May, Egypt had moved one hundred thousand of its own troops plus one thousand tanks and five hundred

---

56   See Martin Gilbert, *Israel, A History* (London: Black Swan, 1998), at pp. 366–367.

heavy guns into the Sinai "buffer zone".[57] The avowed objective was the "extermination of Zionist existence"[58] and the "annihilation" of the "Zionist presence"[59] in Israel.

Shortly after the outbreak of war, Jordan also declared war on Israel. These declarations of war gave rise to the right of military self-defense and legitimized the recapture of the territories Israel had lost in 1948. First, Israel was not acquiring territory as an aggressor, but rather in a defensive war which, like its War of Independence nineteen years earlier, had been forced upon it by the surrounding Arab nations desiring to annihilate it. Secondly, the recaptured areas were a part of the territory rightfully restored to Israel in fulfilment of the Mandate for Palestine.

In fact, after returning the Sinai to Egypt in the peace agreement of 26 March 1979, the territory under Israeli control was almost identical to that which comprised the Mandate for Palestine allotted to it west of the River Jordan in 1922. Israel ultimately also withdrew from the Gaza Strip, on 12 September 2005, but did not transfer control to any other State. Thus, legally, the Gaza Strip remains part of Israel's territory, even though it is not occupied by it at this time.

3. THE "PALESTINIAN" IDENTITY

Something that is largely overlooked in the current debate is the point to which equitable resolutions to the issues of today's Israeli / Arab Palestinian conflict is exacerbated by linguistic hyperbole, factual distortion or pure political maneuvering and calculated rhetoric.

Take for example the word "*Palestinians*" itself. "Palestine" is actually a land the Jews have called "*Eretz-Israel*" (the "Land of Israel") for over three thousand years. The name "Palestine" was actually first applied in Greek and Roman texts. At the time of the San Remo decision and the resulting Mandate for Palestine, the territory then known as "Palestine" was attributed *exclusively* to the Jewish people for the "*reconstitution*" of their national home. Indeed, this was the very purpose of the Mandate for Palestine and its precursor the Balfour Declaration. While care was taken to protect the rights of Arab inhabitants, the Jews alone were the people singled out for the creation of a national home within the territory then known as

---

57   See Martin Gilbert, *Atlas of the Arab-Israeli Conflict*, 6th ed. (Oxford: Oxford University Press, 1993), at p. 67.

58   The Voice of the Arabs radio station, 18 May 1967, as recorded in Isi Leibler, *The Case For Israel* (Australia: The Globe Press, 1972), at p. 60.

59   Syrian Defense Minister Hafez Assad, 20 May 1967, as recorded in *ibid*.

Palestine. This fact is seriously clouded by the linguistic extension of the name "Palestinian" solely to the present-day remnant and descendants of those Arabs who fled or otherwise left the territory of the former greater Palestine (see next section).

"Palestine" was the name applied to the entire mandated territory at the time that Israel came under the League Mandate (i.e. *all* Jewish inhabitants of that territory were equally "Palestinians"). This means that when the Mandate was created there were effectively both "Palestinian Jews" and "Palestinian Arabs", as well as other inhabitants of the territory.

At the time of the Mandate, it would have been more accurate to refer to "Palestinian Jews" and "Palestinian Arabs" (along with the various other non-Jewish inhabitants). But owing to the creation of the State of Israel, the Palestinian Jews reclaimed their ancient name of "Israelis" while the non-Jews (mainly but not all Arabs) continued under the name "Palestinians", with the foreseeable result that they are now viewed as being the rightful inhabitants of the Land.

Thus by virtue of word association, the strong and distinct but erroneous impression is created that it is the (Arab) "Palestinians" who are the real "titleholders" to the territory and that they have been displaced by an aggressive foreign occupying power with no natural or historical claim to the land. In actual fact, the Land called "Palestine" covers territory that the Jews have called the "Holy Land" since well before the name "Palestine" was first used by the Greeks and Romans.

The truth is that the territory once known as "Palestine" has never—either since this name was applied or before—been an Arab nation or been designated to become a sovereign Arab nation. Yet this nomenclature carries with it great psychological impact, with the inference that it is the former Arab inhabitants of Palestine that are the *true* "Palestinians", that they therefore uniquely *belong* in "Palestine" as a distinct "people", and that they have been displaced from territory that was *their* ancestral heritage (although they controlled territory there for only twenty-two years), rather than that of the Jewish "Palestinians" who in actual fact inhabited the Land for thousands of years and had no other "home".

4. THE "REFUGEE" QUESTION

A simple but long-accepted legal definition of *refugee* is "a person who flees or is expelled from a country, esp. because of persecution, and seeks haven in another country"[60] It must be recalled that the principal 1948 "refugee problem" was the direct result of the invasion of ultimately all the Arab League nations[61] upon the termination of the British Mandate and the resulting declaration of independence creating the modern State of Israel,[62] *not* as a result of any policy or practice of systematic persecution of Palestinian Arabs by Palestinian Jews / Israelis.

The new Jewish State had been quickly recognized by the Soviet Union, the United States and many other countries, but not by the surrounding Arab States, which immediately attacked the newborn State of Israel, resulting in the predictable outflow of Palestinian refugees—both Jewish and Arab. The Arab States provided little help to Palestinians who became refugees as the result of their own invasion. It was only Jordan, with understandably the largest Palestinian refugee community in the world, that early on extended full citizenship to all Palestinians who fled across the river into Jordan or who remained in the western areas of Palestine controlled by Jordan. Yet even Jordan—itself, after all, former Palestine and already home to many Palestinians—later revoked many Palestinian refugee citizenships, regarded by many to be in contravention of international law and human rights.

Further, it should be emphasized that Arab Palestinians were not the only ones forced to flee the nascent State of Israel under the multipronged Arab attack. Jewish inhabitants themselves were forced to flee from their long-desired and at-last-acquired national home. From Jerusalem alone, 25 percent (c. 25,000) of the *Jewish* population fled, and their synagogues were destroyed by the invaders. The latter act actually constitutes Arab persecution of Jews in their own land, in addition to the threat to Jewish lives. Families of *all* inhabitants of the land, independent of race, religion or language, fled to escape the ravages of war. (Some of the wealthier Arab inhabitants actually left the country *prior* to the outbreak of war, on the inside knowledge of what was about to occur.[63] Indeed, "[m]any Arabs were encouraged to leave by their own political leaders, who promised them that they would soon be able to return to their homes, once Israel had been destroyed".[64])

---

60   Bryan Garner, ed., *Black's Law Dictionary*, 8th ed. (Thomson West, 2004).
61   See Part II, section 1, *supra*.
62   See Part I, section 10, note 55 and accompanying text, *supra*.
63   See Letter 1355 from Howard Grief to Donna Bank of 23 January 2011.
64   See Gilbert, *Atlas of the Arab-Israeli Conflict, supra* note 57, at p. 47.

In addition to refugees of whatever description fleeing a newly reborn Israel under siege, the Jewish people suddenly found themselves subject to a new wave of persecution in Arab and other Muslim lands where there was *no* war waging. On 16 May 1948, two days after statehood was declared by Israel, the *New York Times* quoted a UN Economic and Social Council report as revealing that: *"The very survival of the Jewish communities in certain Arab and Moslem countries is in serious danger, unless preventive action is taken without delay"*. Indeed, Israel's declaration of independence caused a surge of "premeditated state-sponsored" persecution of Jewish populations in Arab countries on such a scale that some nine hundred thousand Jews were obliged to flee from their homes in Arab nations "from Casablanca to Karachi",[65] thus becoming "refugees" to the full "letter" of the definition—*a fleeing or expelled persecuted people*. This side of the refugee question is rarely heard of.

The point here is not one-upmanship. The point here is that these thousands of Jewish refugees, reportedly more numerous than their Arab counterparts,[66] have long since reintegrated, been reabsorbed into society and resumed normal and productive lives. This is apart from the fact that since that time, Jordan (i.e. Arab Palestine) has actually *expelled* Jews, which not only makes them true refugees by definition but which is in direct contravention to Article 15 of the Mandate for Palestine. Yet these are never heard mentioned in the refugee rhetoric. Article 25, which enabled the establishment of Trans-Jordan for the Palestinian Arabs and ultimately the sovereign State of Jordan, provides that "no action shall be taken which is inconsistent with the provisions of Articles 15, 16, and 18". Article 15 reads in part:

> No discrimination of any kind shall be made between the inhabitants of Palestine on the ground of race, religion or language. No person shall be excluded from Palestine on the sole ground of his religious belief.

This applies to *all* of former Palestine.

The present plight of all those living in refugee camps is truly pitiable and rightfully arouses the compassion of the world. As recently

---

65   See Eli E. Hertz, "UN Resolution 194: Arab Leaders Point to Resolution 194 as Proof that Arab Refugees Have a 'Right to Return'—False", 13 August 2009, http://www.myths-andfacts.org/Conflict/10/ Resolution-194.pdf.

66   See Grief, Letter 1355, *supra* note 63.

as August of 2011, a refugee camp in Syria came under sustained assault from Syrian Government forces. An UNRWA spokesperson said that "many people around the world were shocked by the images of unarmed refugees being shot at as they fled from their homes, amid the firing on their refugee camp".[67] This was Arabs firing on Arab refugees.

The fact is that most of the Palestinians identified as "refugees" are well over a generation away from the events that caused the foregoing generation to flee. Reportedly some 90 percent of the "refugees" now living as such never, themselves, inhabited or fled the Land of Israel.[68] For the most part, the latest generation of those "refugees" situated outside of the Land does not even know Israel; it was never their home.[69]

There are twenty-one sovereign Arab nations, most of which have already enjoyed statehood for generations, with the collective capacity and resources to have long since welcomed their Arab brothers to be reabsorbed into their own vast homelands, particularly those lands carved out for them at the same moment in history that Palestine was being set apart for the Jewish national home. Indeed, *in addition to the other San Remo mandated territories that gained statehood before Israel and could have absorbed their Arab brothers, Trans-Jordan was partitioned off* specially *for the Palestinian Arabs, and in territory originally envisaged for the Jewish national home. This already furnished a legitimate "new State" for the Arabs within the very territory of "Palestine" as it was then known.*

The "refugees" are in effect being inhumanely "used" for a political cause that is not inherently their own. Their plight has been "high-profiled" for over six decades, and prolonged interminably as a symbol and silent weapon for political and territorial gain in the interest of a further incursion into the Jewish mandated territory. This is not mere supposition. Arab leaders over the years have *expressly stated* that the Palestinian refugees are maintained as a weapon against Israel. These statements and corresponding policy moves speak very powerfully for themselves. For example: [70]

---

67   See UN News Service, 19 August 2011, "UN provides emergency help to Palestinian refugees displaced by fighting in Syria", http://www.un.org/apps/news/story.asp?NewsID=39342&Cr =Syria&Cr1.

68   See Grief, Letter 1355, *supra* note 63.

69   Regions with significant "1948 refugee" populations outside of Israel (sometimes known as "present absentees") and the Gaza Strip and "West Bank" are Jordan, Lebanon and Syria.

70   The following bulleted quotes are found in Gilbert, *Atlas of the Arab-Israeli Conflict*,

- In April 1949, at the UN Palestine Conciliation Commission at Lausanne, Israel offered to repatriate one hundred thousand Arab refugees within the framework of a general settlement. The Arab delegations rejected the offer.

- In 1950 the United Nations Relief and Works Agency (UNRWA) proposed resettling the Arab refugees in Sinai, Jordan and Syria, but the Arab Governments rejected this proposal.

- In 1952 the UN Refugee Rehabilitation Fund offered the Arab States $200 million to find "homes and jobs" for the refugees. The Arab States used some of the money for relief work, but did not even apply for the greater part of the fund.

- Al Siyyad, Beirut, 6 April 1950: "The return of the refugees....forming a powerful fifth column for the day of revenge and reckoning".

- Abd Allah Al-Yafi, Lebanese Prime Minister, 29 April 1966: "The day of realisation of the Arab hope for the return of the refugees to Palestine means the liquidation of Israel".[71]

- Radio Cairo, 19 July 1957: "The refugees are the cornerstone in the Arab struggle against Israel. The refugees are the armaments of the Arabs and Arab nationalism".

The use of "refugees" as political pawns—innocent victims of the deliberate perpetuation of their refugee status, generation after generation, while their numbers and the related financial burden on the international community continue to increase exponentially—is unique in human history. The 1948 refugees and their descendants

supra note 57, at p. 54.

71   On the Right of Return as applied to the Arab Palestinians, see Eli E. Hertz, "UN Resolution 194: Arab Leaders Point to Resolution 194 as Proof that Arab Refugees Have a 'Right to Return'—False", 13 August 2009, http://www.mythsandfacts.org/Conflict/10/Resolution-194.pdf.

now reportedly number into the 5 to 6 millions,[72] and the issue is being kept alive through simply prolonging the use of the term "refugees" into every succeeding generation. It is UNRWA and not international law that has conferred refugee status on the descendants of the 1948 refugees. International law has never had to grapple with the question of the perpetual "inheritance" of refugee status.

5. THE "1967 LINES"

As a point of reference for a new Palestinian State, there is constant mention of withdrawal to the "1967 borders". Firstly, this terminology is legally incorrect. The word "borders" is generally used in international law to mean "national boundaries", which the "1967 lines" most decidedly are not. The definition of a "border" under international law is "a boundary between one nation (or a political subdivision [of that nation]) and another".[73] No such national boundaries have ever been established for the reborn State of Israel. The 1967 so-called "boundaries" are purely *military* no-cross lines, *expressly* repeated in *numerous* Israeli-Palestinian agreements to neither represent national borders nor prejudice the future bilateral negotiation of same.

The term "1967 lines" is used to indicate the lines from which the Israeli military moved into territory to counter the attacks that initiated hostilities on 5 June 1967 (the Six-Day War). They do not—nor did they ever—represent national boundaries, nor have they ever even been defined as national borders in any legal document pertaining to "Palestine" or Israel. Thus such "lines" construed as "borders" can be derived from neither "history, law nor fact".[74]

These "lines" (also called the "Green Line" because they were originally marked out on a map with a green marker) are armistice

---

72 These figures come from Benny Morris, "Exposing Abbas—Why Israel?", 23 May 2011. In general, refugee figures are unreliable, since persons in need of support who became refugees as a result of the 1967 conflict have been added to the roles by UNRWA. Moreover, deaths are often not reported so as not to reduce aid for the family of the deceased. Other refugees are from time to time registered with the Palestinian refugees, as well as other needy individuals who have never been refugees, at the discretion of UNRWA. (See e.g. UNGA doc. A/2171 of 30 June 1952, General Assembly Official Records (GAOR): Seventh Session, Supp. No. 13 (A/2171), New York, 1952.)
73 *Black's Law Dictionary, supra* note 60.
74 See Alan Baker, "The Fallacy of the '1967 Borders'—No Such Borders Ever Existed", *Jerusalem Issue Brief*, Vol. 10, No. 17, 21 December 2010, at p. 1. (Amb. Allen Baker is former Legal Advisor to Israel's Foreign Ministry.)

demarcation lines, resulting from the armistice agreements signed between Israel and its Arab neighbors Egypt, Jordan, Syria and Lebanon in 1949, following the 1948 War of Independence. These 1949 armistice lines were no more than lines separating armies and were dictated exclusively by military considerations. They were never intended to do more than delimit the lines that the military forces of each affected party were committed not to cross "during the transition to permanent peace in Palestine"[75] and until permanent borders could eventually be negotiated between the respective parties. This *transitional, provisional* character of the cease fire lines was emphasized in all of the respective armistice agreements. They remained valid only until the outbreak of the 1967 Six-Day War. Accordingly, the most accurate, appropriate and transparent term for the "Green Line" would be the *"pre-1967 armistice lines"*. Falsely linking them with the 1967 war—where lost territory was recovered by the Israeli Defense Forces—by calling them "1967 borders" instead of 1949 armistice lines, fosters the erroneous notion that these are ill-gotten *national* "borders", thus highly prejudicing the issue and its outcome.

The exact language of the Israel-Jordan Armistice Agreement, signed on 13 April 1949 and typifying all the respective agreements, reads:

> The basic purpose of the Armistice Demarcation Lines is to delineate the lines beyond which the armed forces of the respective Parties shall not move.[76] … [as] agreed upon by the Parties *without prejudice to future territorial settlements or boundary lines or to claims of either Party relating thereto* [emphasis added].[77]

All of the 1949 armistice agreements expressly provide that such lines have no political or legal significance that could in any way prejudice future arrangements or agreements under international law. Nothing has ever changed this. On 28 May 1967 Professor Mughraby wrote in the Beirut *Daily Star*:

> Israel is the only State in the world which has no legal boundaries except the natural one the Mediterranean provides. The rest are nothing more than armistice lines

---

75   See UN Security Council Resolution 62 of 16 November 1948.
76   Israel-Jordan Armistice Agreement, Article IV(2).
77   *Ibid.*, Article VI(9).

[and] can never be considered political or territorial boundaries.[78]

In the aftermath of the Six-Day War, even the United Nations was forced to recognize that the armistice lines were not appropriate for the assurance of protection against aggression. Accordingly, UN Security Council Resolution 242 of 22 November 1967, which formed the "conceptual foundation"[79] for an eventual peace settlement, is aimed at guaranteeing that all States in the region have "safe and secure" borders. Even Resolution 242, which has been interpreted in many different ways, did not seek to determine where those boundaries should be drawn.

The U.S. ambassador to the UN at the time, former Supreme Court Justice Arthur Goldberg, pointed out in 1973 that the fact that the resolution omitted to call for total withdrawal is in recognition of the fact that *"Israel's prior frontiers had proven to be notably insecure"*. Even the Soviet delegate to the UN, Vasily Kuznetsov, who fought against the final text, conceded that the resolution gave Israel the right to "withdraw its forces only to those lines it considers appropriate".[80]

Lord Caradon, the British UN Ambassador at the time and the resolution's principal drafter, who introduced it to the Council, stated unequivocally in 1974 that:

> It would have been wrong to demand that Israel return to its positions of June 4, 1967, because those positions were undesirable and artificial.[81]

Eugene V. Rostow, U.S. Undersecretary of State for Political Affairs in 1967 and one of the drafters of the Resolution, stated in 1990 that it and subsequent Security Council Resolution 338:

> ...rest on two principles, Israel may administer the territory until its Arab neighbors make peace; and when peace is made, Israel should withdraw to "secure and

---

78   See Baker, *supra* note 74, at p. 4.
79   Eli E. Hertz, "No Return to the 1967 Borders", Myth and Fact, 29 April 2011.
80   As excerpted and edited from and cited in Danny Ayalon, "Israel's Right in the 'Disputed' Territories", *Wall Street Journal*, Opinion Europe, 20 May 2011. (Amb. Daniel Ayalon is the Deputy Foreign Minister of Israel.).
81   *Ibid.*

recognized borders", which need not be the same as the
Armistice Demarcation Lines of 1949.[82]

Even the "Road Map",[83] initiated by the "Quartet" (the European
Union, the United Nations, the Russian Federation and the United
States) in 2003 refers to *the still outstanding need to negotiate permanent borders.* This document not only puts off the "borders" question until the second and third phases of implementation (and only
then if a responsible Arab Palestinian leadership has been elected)
but it calls initially for only "provisional borders" pending a permanent settlement with "final status" borders in the third stage, and
requiring international recognition.

In a word, the 1967 lines are *not* "borders" at all, and this word
should not be used to create and perpetuate the impression that Israel
has illegally transgressed the borders of another State, when this is
clearly not the case.

6. THE DISPUTED TERRITORIES

Any discussion of the so-called "occupied territories" has become
all but politically "taboo". Nonetheless, one or two points need to
be borne in mind in the ongoing debate. Suffice it to say that the
sentiment and political and even legal rhetoric is very strong here.
Positions taken on both sides are adamant. But it must be acknowledged that the widespread use of the words "occupied territory" with
an implied sense of "*belligerent* occupation" rather than simply "disputed territory" (which in fact it is) has a major psychological impact
that can result in real and even legal ramifications.

Furthermore, this language and what it (falsely) tends to connote (i.e. "belligerent occupation") totally ignores the international
treaty language of "reconstituted", as contained in the Mandate for
Palestine. *Reconstituted* territory *precludes* "belligerent occupation", even if permanent national borders have yet to be negotiated.
A State cannot, by definition, be a "belligerent occupying power" in
a territory that is being "reconstituted" in its name, according to
the provisions of a legally binding instrument of international law.
The territory in question is occupied *Israeli* territory, *not* occupied

---

82   *Ibid.*
83   "Performance-Based Roadmap to a Permanent Two-State Solution to the Israeli-
Palestinian Conflict" of 30 April 2003.

Palestinian territory. This is a perfectly acceptable status under international law and brings with it certain legal responsibilities, on the part of the occupier, toward the inhabitants of the occupied territory. The definition of "occupied territory" in international law is given in Article 42 of the Hague Regulations:

> Territory is considered occupied when it is actually placed under the authority of the hostile army. The occupation extends only to the territory where such authority has been established and can be exercised.[84]

It could be argued that Israel's "occupation" of the disputed territories does not fall under the classic definition of military occupation at all, in that such "occupation occurs when a belligerent State invades the territory of another State with the intention of holding the territory at least temporarily".[85] The territory that Israel reclaimed in 1967 was never rightfully "the territory of another State", nor did Israel obtain it by war of aggression, as noted above. Indeed, it was territory that had been specifically designated for a *Jewish* national home, under the legally binding League of Nations Mandate for Palestine in 1922. Despite the *eastern* three quarters of the territory then known as "Palestine" being partitioned off (from territory originally designated in 1920 by the San Remo resolution for the Jewish national home, with borders to be determined), in order to form the Arab territory of Trans-Jordan, nothing has altered the final 1922 League-approved Mandate *west* of the Jordan or assigned that territory to any State other than Israel.

Under international law, the applicability of the legal regime on "*belligerent* occupation" (often popularly but erroneously assumed to be the meaning here) enters into effect "as soon as the armed forces of a *foreign* power have secured effective control over a territory that is *not its own*".[86] Again, the territory in question here—with exact borders still to be delineated—is that which was set apart for the

---

84 Hague Convention Number IV Respecting the Laws and Customs of War on Land, 18 October 1907, Regulations, Article 42.
85 West's Encyclopedia of American Law, 2nd ed., c. 2008, The Gale Group, Inc.
86 Amnesty International (AI), http://web.amnesty.org/library/index/eng…..While this definition of "belligerent occupation" as articulated by AI refers to "Iraq: Responsibilities of the occupying powers", it is of some interest to note that when referring to Israel and "Occupied Palestinian Territories" in a number of position papers, AI has no regard to this definition.

national home of the Jewish people by the Supreme Council of the Principal Allied Powers at San Remo in 1920.

It is the Regulations of the Hague Conventions of 1907 together with the 1949 Fourth Geneva Convention[87] that form the international legal regime relating to military occupation. Under these Conventions, the occupying power assumes, for a limited period, responsibility for the security and well-being of the occupied territory's inhabitants. The military authorities have the obligation under international law to maintain public order, respect private property, and honor individual liberties. Particularly with regard to the maintenance of public order, armed forces are the normal enforcement requisite. In the language of Article 4 of the Geneva Convention (IV), all civilians in occupied territories are the "protected persons" whose rights are to be safeguarded.

Under the current circumstances, it is the responsibility of the Israel Defense Forces (IDF) to maintain peace and order and to assure the safety and security of both the Jewish and non-Jewish populations, the 1949 armistice lines serving as *temporary* "borders" having proved to be insecure and indefensible.

Article 43 of the Hague Regulations states that:

> The authority of the legitimate power having in fact passed into the hands of the occupant, the latter shall take all the measures in his power to restore, and ensure, as far as possible, public order and safety, while respecting, unless absolutely prevented, the laws in force in the country.[88]

Note that occupation takes place when "*the authority of the legitimate power [has] in fact passed into the hands of the occupant*". It is quite clear that there was no "legitimate power" in the "West Bank" from 1949 to 1967, since this territory was illegally annexed by Jordan, with no international recognition (other than Britain and, possibly, Pakistan) and with no recognition even from other Arab countries.[89]

The Deputy Foreign Minister of Israel, Danny Ayalon, points out that the land now known as the "West Bank" cannot be considered

---

87   Convention (IV) relative to the Protection of Civilian Persons in Time of War, Geneva, 12 August 1949 (International Committee of the Red Cross, Geneva).
88   Hague Convention, *supra* note 84, Article 43.
89   Appreciation to S. Benzimra, note 3 *supra*, e-mail of 15 June 2011.

"occupied" in the legal sense of the word, as it had not attained recognized sovereignty before Israel's conquest. He goes on to recall that, contrary to some beliefs, there has never been a Palestinian State, and no other nation has ever established Jerusalem as its capital, despite its once having been under Islamic control for hundreds of years.[90]

While clear "title" to the "West Bank" is adamantly contested on both sides, referring to it as "[belligerent] occupied territory" overtly prejudices the just resolution of the conflict.

7. The Settlements Question

Of course an immediate corollary to the issue of claims to the disputed territory is that of "settlements". The issue of the legality of the Israeli policy on settlements is arguably the most high-profile and contentious issue calling for resolution in the overall Israeli-Palestinian debate. There are as many opinions as there are sides to the issue, and—as in all areas of the delicate questions surrounding this highly valued land— there is no "cut and dried" legal solution.

Beginning after the 1967 war, when Jews started returning to their historic heartland in the "West Bank"—or Judea and Samaria as the territory had been known around the world for two thousand years prior to its renaming by the Jordanians—the issue of settlements arose. U.S. Undersecretary of State Rostow found no legal impediment to Jewish settlement in these territories, maintaining that the original Mandate for Palestine still applies to the "West Bank". Rostow stated:

> [T]he Jewish right of settlement in Palestine west of the Jordan River, that is, in Israel, the West Bank, Jerusalem, was made unassailable. That right has never been terminated and cannot be terminated except by a recognized peace between Israel and its neighbors. There is no subsequent legally binding instrument pertaining to the territory at issue that has nullified this right of Jewish settlement.[91]

The sensitivities surrounding this question are exacerbated by the very fact that the legality/illegality of such settlements is based on

---

90   This and the following para. are excerpted from Ayalon, *supra* note 80.
91   See *ibid.*

factors that may not follow prescribed international law norms but
rather are complicated by the unique nature of the Israeli settlements
in particular.

For example, while it is often claimed that such settlements violate Article 49 of the Geneva Convention (IV), the inclusion of this
Article in the Convention had a different purpose altogether than to
govern circumstances such as those existing in present-day Israel.
Specifically, the intent of the drafters was to prevent belligerent occupying powers from deporting civilian populations, against their will
and for political purposes, into a territory they were belligerently
occupying.

According to the International Committee of the Red Cross:

> It is intended to prevent a practice adopted during the
> Second World War by certain Powers, which transferred
> portions of their own population to occupied territory for
> political and racial reasons or in order, as they claimed,
> to colonize those territories. Such transfers worsened the
> economic situation of the native population and endan-
> gered their separate existence as a race.

Thus the drafters' intent was that of *protecting vulnerable civilians
in times of armed conflict* by creating an international legal instrument that would declare as unlawful all *coerced deportation* such
as that suffered by more than forty million Germans, Soviets, Poles,
Ukrainians, Hungarians and others, immediately after the Second
World War.

The exact wording of the relevant paragraph (6) of Article 49 reads:

> The Occupying Power shall not deport or transfer parts of
> its own civilian population into the territory it occupies.

In the case of Israel, under international law as embodied in the
Mandate for Palestine, Jews were *permitted* and even *encouraged*
to settle in *every part* of Palestine; they were *not* deported or forc-
ibly transferred. Accordingly, calling the "East Jerusalem", Judea and
Samaria Israeli settlements "illegal" is not an apt application of the
Fourth Geneva Convention.

The fact that the original intent of Article 49 of the Convention
was not applicable to the Israeli case for settlements is demonstrated

by the perceived need to insert into the text of the Article—at the initiation of the Arab States, during the negotiations of the 1988 Rome Statute of the International Criminal Court— of the language "*directly or indirectly*" (making into a war crime the "transfer, *directly or indirectly*, by the Occupying Power of parts of its own civilian population into the territory it occupies" (emphasis added).[92] Yet the continued reference to the Geneva Convention (IV) by the international community, when it comes to judging the legal status of the Israeli settlements under international law, ignores the history, legal framework and negotiating environment surrounding Judea and Samaria (the so-called "West Bank").

In 2010, Palestinian delegates at the United Nations drafted a resolution declaring that Israeli settlements are "illegal and constitute a major obstacle to the achievement of peace". The very fact that it was deemed necessary to articulate this in a resolution, itself implies that this fact is not clearly established under the conventional international legal order.

This sensitive and highly contentious question of settlements is specifically among those slated for the "*permanent status*" negotiations called for in the Interim Agreement concluded at Oslo on 28 September 1995[93] and still to be held between Israelis and Arab Palestinians. Such negotiations on this all-important item should not be circumvented by transferring them to the arena of UN General Assembly resolutions, or by bypassing all organizational channels to directly engage the public forum and the international community at large, thus evading and ignoring international legal responsibility.

8. THE QUESTION OF JERUSALEM

In considering the implications of a possible unilateral declaration of a Palestinian State with "East Jerusalem" as its capital, of utmost significance is the fact that, to the Jewish people, "East Jerusalem" *is* Jerusalem. The walls of Jerusalem in A.D. 100, in Crusader times and in the mid-nineteenth century are virtually the same as the boundaries of the Old City (within "East Jerusalem") today. This means that

---

92   Article 8, para. 2(b)(viii).
93   The Israeli-Palestinian Interim Agreement on the West Bank and the Gaza Strip of 28 September 1995, known variously as the "Interim Agreement", or "Oslo II", or the "Taba accord", was the second phase of the process that had begun with the establishment of the Palestinian Authority in Gaza and Jericho in May 1994, setting the stage for the permanent status talks to begin by May 1996.

if "East Jerusalem" were to be partitioned off to become the capital of a Palestinian State, the Jewish people would actually lose their eternal capital and sovereign control over their eternally sacred holy sites, including their most holy Temple.

Under Israeli control, every area of the country, including the Temple Mount, is open to all "races, religions or languages". If Jerusalem were to be incorporated into a Palestinian State, the large Jewish population of "East Jerusalem" (including the Old City, which is virtually equivalent to the "City of Jerusalem" up to the mid-nineteenth century) would be forced to leave their homes, since the Palestinian Authority (PA) chairman Abbas, has stated that he will not allow Jews to live in a Palestinian State. In a July 2010 news item we read:

> Almost no notice was taken of [a pre-peace-negotiations] decision that the PA chairman Mahmoud Abbas revealed, as he announced clearly that if a Palestinian Authority state is created in Judea and Samaria [the so-called "West Bank"], no Israeli citizen will be allowed to set foot inside. The PA chairman also stated that he would block any Jewish soldiers from serving with an international force stationed on PA-controlled land. "I will never allow a single Israeli to live among us on Palestine's land", Abbas declared.[94]

This would be reminiscent of 1948 when, upon the collective Arab invasion, some 25,000 Jews were forced to flee Jerusalem. That, at the time, represented 25 percent of the Jewish population living in Jerusalem. Today there are reportedly an estimated 225,000 Jews living in eastern Jerusalem.[95] The apartheid policy of a new Palestinian State with "East Jerusalem" as its capital would force all Jews to evacuate their homes in that part of the capital.[96]

This is not unprecedented. Jews have not been allowed to buy land or even to live in Jordan, a land originally carved out of the

---

94   "Arab League Tries to Score Points for Abbas, 'Endorses' Talks", Arutz Sheva, 29 July 2010, http://www.israelnationalnews.com/News/News.aspx/138856
95   Chaim Silberstein, MBA, founder and president of "Keep Jerusalem", a public advocacy organization, speaking at "Together for the Sake of Jerusalem" conference on the recognition of the international legal rights of the Jewish People and the State of Israel to the city of Jerusalem, 29-31 August 2011, Musiksaal, Basel, Switzerland.
96   See text accompanying note 94, *supra.*

Palestine that was designated by the Principal Allied Powers in 1920 to provide a national home for the dispersed Jewish people. Moreover, the current stated policy in the bid for an additional State for Arab Palestinians within the legally founded Jewish mandated territory west of the river Jordan likewise vehemently excludes Jewish inhabitants—even those who are already well-established there. This is in direct contravention to Article 15 of the Mandate for Palestine, still in effect to this day in these relevant parts. Furthermore, any such discrimination/persecution and outright expulsion would make true Jewish refugees out of legitimate homeland inhabitants by replacing them with the Arab "refugee" descendants, whose "refugee" status is quite overtly perpetuated for this very purpose, as outlined above.

Throughout history, whenever Jerusalem has been under Jewish or Christian control, it has *always* been the capital for the Jewish people. Conversely, whenever Jerusalem has *not* been under Jewish or Christian control, Jerusalem has *never* been the capital (for the foreign occupants). *Other* cities have *always* been named the capital under Islamic control. Indeed, when Muslims bow to pray, they face Mecca, even if that means turning their 'hind parts' toward Jerusalem, and, if in Jerusalem, to the Temple Mount, which is their practice irrespective even of the presence there of the Al-Aqsa Mosque and the Dome of the Rock.

There are many differing opinions—even among international lawyers—on the legal status, or proposed legal status, of the city of Jerusalem.[97] It is arguably the most desired piece of "real estate" on the face of the earth, owing to the sanctity of its Holy Places and to age-old rivalries for control. This situation is further complicated by the fact that it is frequently exploited for political objectives.

It is of some note that neither the Balfour Declaration nor the Mandate for Palestine made separate reference to Jerusalem. This in itself would indicate that the Mandate does not single out this city for special treatment, other than for the "Holy Places". It is in fact the universally recognized sanctity and "common heritage" of the Holy Places that gave rise to Part III of Resolution 181(II) of 29 November 1947 (the "Partition Resolution"), as concerns Jerusalem. This Resolution recommended in the relevant provisions that a "governor" be appointed by the United Nations to administer the Holy City as a *corpus separatum*. This recommendation was accepted by

---

97   See e.g. Lapidoth, *supra* note 1, from which the following factual details are also largely derived.

the national leadership of the Jewish community of Palestine but categorically rejected by the Arabs, who responded by initiating attacks on Jewish towns and villages, including the Jewish communities in Jerusalem.[98]

In 1949, following renewed debate in the UN General Assembly on the question of Jerusalem, Israeli Prime Minister David Ben-Gurion announced in the Knesset that Jerusalem was an *"inseparable part of the State of Israel"* and its *"Eternal Capital"*.[99] His pronouncement was approved by the Israeli Parliament. Similarly, following the Camp David conference, Israeli Prime Minister Menachem Begin pronounced that *"Jerusalem is one city, indivisible, the capital of the State of Israel"*, while Egyptian President Anwar Sadat proclaimed that *"Arab Jerusalem is an integral part of the West Bank... and should be under Arab sovereignty"*. Note that, for the sovereign State of Israel, Jerusalem *is* the indivisible capital of the State of Israel, whereas in the counter statement with reference to the "West Bank", which is *not* sovereign territory belonging to the Arabs, it is not a case of *"is"* but a concept of *"should be"*. There is no valid or justifiable legal claim to separating this portion of Jerusalem from Israeli territory granted under the Mandate for Palestine. (Every nation has the right to designate its own national capital within its own sovereign territory.)

While Jerusalem was mentioned in several declarations/agreements in 1993–1995,[100] it was not on the agenda of the 1991 Madrid Middle East Peace Conference, nor was it mentioned in the controversial UN Security Council Resolution 242 of 22 November 1967 calling for the withdrawal of Israeli armed forces from territories occupied in June 1967, *conditional on Arab belligerence coming to an end*. Nor was it named in the Framework for Peace in the Middle East, agreed in the 1978 Camp David Accords between Israel and Egypt. In the latter case, Jerusalem was indeed on the agenda, but was left out of the actual Accords, owing to the inability of the two parties to resolve their fundamental differences on the highly loaded issue.

In 1980, a new law concerning Jerusalem was adopted by the

---

98   See *ibid.*
99   See *Record of Knesset Proceedings*, December 1949, Vol. 3, at pp. 220–226, 281–287.
100 See e.g. the 1993 Declaration of Principles on Interim Self-Government Arrangements ("Declaration of Principles"), the 1995 Interim Agreement [*supra* note 93], and the 1994 Israel-Jordan Peace Treaty.

Knesset: the Basic Law: Jerusalem, Capital of Israel.[101] The Basic Law in fact contains no new principles; it only codifies the situation as it has long existed and has persistently been declared and effectuated: (1) that "Jerusalem, complete and united, is the capital of Israel" (sect. 1); (2) that it is "the seat of the President of the State, the Knesset, the Government, and the Supreme Court" (sect. 2); and (3) that the Holy Places shall be protected (sect. 3). It additionally commits to the "development" and "prosperity" of the city (sect. 4). There is nothing in this language, content or actuality that runs contrary to the international legal rights of a sovereign State.

Finally, as expressed by Jerusalem scholar Dr. Gauthier, "the failure of the Camp David Summit of July 2000 very much underlined the significance of the question of Jerusalem and its Old City. It was evident that the positions of Israel and the Palestinians regarding the Old City were irreconcilable".[102]

Pending a resolution of this volatile issue, the non-Jewish residents of the eastern part of Jerusalem (so-called "East Jerusalem") have, since the birth of the State of Israel, enjoyed the status of *permanent residents of Israel*, guaranteeing the protection of their existing rights and endowing them with social and cultural benefits, consistent with the Mandate for Palestine that provided for the safeguarding of civil and religious rights of non-Jews in all of the territory designated at that time as "Palestine". This has ongoing application in the modern State of Israel. In fact, upon achieving statehood, Israeli citizenship was also made available to such residents, through the normal legal process of "naturalization".

9. Commitments to "Permanent Status" Negotiations

After the Six-Day War, as noted above, UN Security Council Resolution 242 affirmed the *right* to "secure and recognized boundaries".[103] Although there was *no provision calling for a return to the 1949 armistice demarcation lines*, the intention was that a peace settlement would follow that would include the negotiation of

---

101   Passed by the Knesset on the 17th Av, 5740 (30 July 1980), *published in*: Sefer Ha-Chukkim No. 980 of the 23rd Av, 5740 (5 August 1980), at p. 186.
102   See Gauthier, *supra* note 12, at p. 848; see also *ibid.*, Chapter XIII, Section I.
103   UN Security Council Resolution 242, 22 November 1967, para. 1(ii).

recognized and defensible national borders to supplant the old provisional armistice lines.

While this was not realized at the time, the basic reciprocal undertaking by the Palestinian and Israeli leaderships to negotiate borders between their respective territories was given formal confirmation by Yasser Arafat, and in turn by his deputy and later replacement Mahmoud Abbas, as well as by Sa'eb Erekat, during the groundbreaking Declaration of Principles on Interim Self-Government Arrangements (signed *inter alia* by Abbas) of 13 September 1993. On this date the Palestine Liberation Organization (PLO) and the Government of Israel acknowledged that the negotiations on the "permanent status" of the relationship between them would cover:

> ...remaining issues, including: Jerusalem, refugees, settlements, security arrangements, borders, relations and cooperation with other neighbors, and other issues of common interest.[104]

In a word, the PLO leadership pledged in 1993 to commit virtually *all* the important issues of permanent status to resolution by *negotiations only*. On the eve of the signature of the above declaration, Arafat made the following solemn commitment in a letter to Israeli Prime Minister Yitzhak Rabin:

> The PLO commits itself to the Middle East peace process, and to a peaceful resolution of the conflict between the two sides and declares that *all* outstanding issues relating to permanent status *will be resolved through negotiations* [emphasis added]. [105]

References to "permanent status negotiations" on borders were contained in a series of agreements concluded between the PLO and the Israeli Government over the period of 1993 to 1999. Particularly significant in this respect is the 1995 Interim Agreement (Oslo II)[106]

---

104 Declaration of Principles on Interim Self-Government Arrangements, 13 September 1993, Article V, para. 3, Jewish Virtual Library, http://www.jewishvirtuallibrary.org/jsource/Peace/dop.html.
105 Exchange of letters between Yasser Arafat and Yitzhak Rabin, 9 July 1993, http://www.mfa.gov.il/ MFA/Peace+Process/Guide+to+the+Peace+Process/Israel-PLO+Recognition+-+Exchange+of+Letters+betwe.htm.
106 The Interim Agreement, *supra* note 93.

by which the parties undertook *to not act unilaterally* to alter the status of the territories prior to the results of permanent status negotiations:

> ...*neither side* shall initiate or take *any step* that will *change the status* of the West Bank and the Gaza strip pending the outcome of *the permanent status negotiations* [emphasis added].[107]

This language was repeated in the 1999 Sharm el Sheikh Memorandum[108] (Article 9). The 1995 Interim Agreement also stipulates that:

> ...the [Palestinian] Council *will not have powers and responsibilities in the sphere of foreign relations*, which sphere includes the establishment abroad of embassies, consulates or other types of foreign missions and posts or permitting their establishment in the West Bank or the Gaza Strip, the appointment of or admission of diplomatic and consular staff, and the exercise of diplomatic functions [emphasis added]. [109]

A unilaterally declared Palestinian State would therefore be in breach of commitments embodied in an international legal instrument as well as in publicly declared and published official statements and documents.

Moreover, there must be a formal peace treaty between two legally empowered negotiating partners who mutually recognize one another's existence as legitimate States or international legal entities with all the powers required to exercise diplomatic functions. Accordingly, the members of the Quartet (the EU, Russia, the UN and the U.S.) insist that Israel's negotiating partner meet three basic undertakings prior to statehood talks: (1) to recognize the State of Israel, (2) to

---

107 *Ibid.*, Article XXXI (7)
108 The Sharm el Sheikh Memorandum on Implementation Timeline of Outstanding Commitments of Agreements Signed and the Resumption of Permanent Status Negotiations, 4 September 1999, Jewish Virtual Library, http://www.jewishvirtuallibrary.org/jsource/Peace/sharm0999.html. The aim of this Memorandum was the implementation of the Interim Agreement (*supra* note 93) and of all other agreements between the PLO and Israel since September 1993.
109 The Interim Agreement, *supra* note 93, Article IX (5.a.).

renounce the use of terrorism and violence, and (3) to recognize the validity of previously negotiated Israeli-Palestinian agreements.

Were it not for the above pre-conditions set by the Quartet, Israeli negotiators would find themselves sitting across the negotiating table in the shadow of two extreme antagonists committed to their ultimate if not hasty demise. The (Fatah) PLO Charter[110] calls for the "total liberation" of Palestine and declares that "the struggle will not end until the elimination of the Zionist entity and the [total] liberation of Palestine". (For "total liberation" read: "total takeover of control".) The "liberation" of "Palestine" (including the mandated Jewish territory of the State of Israel) is mentioned twenty-seven times in the thirty-three articles of the PA Charter/Covenant.

In addition, Article 20 of the Charter reads:

> The Balfour Declaration, the Mandate for Palestine, and everything that has been based upon them, are deemed null and void.

The (Hamas) Charter of the Islamic Resistance Movement[111] states that "Israel will exist and will continue to exist until Islam will obliterate it."...[112] Thus it would appear that, "rhetorically", Fatah "recognizes" a "Zionist entity" and "rhetorically" Hamas "recognizes" the "existence" of Israel. But the rhetoric is not a civil one. Neither of these pronouncements bodes well for amicable bilateral negotiations

---

110   The Palestinian National Charter: Resolutions of the Palestine National Council, 1–17 July 1968, as *translated and reproduced in*: "The Avalon Project: Documents in Law, History and Diplomacy", Yale Law School, Lillian Goldman Law Library, online: http://avalon.law.yale.edu/20th_century/plocov.asp. From time to time there is talk of having abrogated certain provisions of the Charter, although it is not clear that the relevant legal requirements for such Charter amendments have been fulfilled. (See http://palwatch.org/main.aspx?fi=711&fld_id=723&doc_id=450.) Recently, the PA chairman called for the Charter to be amended by September 31 [sic] 2011. (See http://www.aljazeerah.info/News/2011/March/28%20n/Abbas%20Moves%20on%20PLO%20Constitution%20Amendments%20to%20Include%20Hamas%20and%20Islamic%20Jihad.htm)—*post* UN General Assembly Annual Session earlier that month where the PA chairman anticipated a vote and Security Council approval to recognize a unilateral declaration of Palestinian statehood. But this would seem to be little more than a superficial appeasement of the outspoken criticisms of this volatile language as contained in a national Charter. It appears that there have been no formal Charter amendments at the time of writing, and, in any case, without a clear change of internal rhetoric and of policy and political practice, a change of words only would tend to ring hollow.

111   The Covenant of the Islamic Resistance Movement, 18 August 1988, as *translated and reproduced in*: ibid.

112   *Ibid.*, Preamble.

leading to territorially contiguous States living peaceably behind shared national borders. Moreover, the two major rival Arab ruling factions, Fatah and Hamas, would have to come into a viable and lasting unity government that could effectively represent the Arab Palestinians.

As recently as 26 August 2011, on the occasion of the Iranian "international Quds Day", an annual show of support for the Palestinian Authority, Iranian President Mahmoud Ahmadinejad, restating the position he outlined after taking office in 2005, proclaimed that Israel is a "tumor" to be wiped off the map and urged Arabs in PA-administered areas not to accept a two-State solution, but to strive for a complete "return" of "Palestine". Ahmadinejad declared to worshipers: *"Recognizing the Palestinian State is not the ultimate goal. It is only one step forward towards liberating the whole of Palestine". "A 'Palestinian State' is only the first step in the destruction of Israel".*[113]

In addition, while the Israeli Government has even offered citizenship to all eligible non-Jewish inhabitants, in addition to the safeguards to the "civil and religious rights of the non-Jewish communities" living in former Palestine, as guaranteed by the Mandate for Palestine, the reverse is not true. It has been openly declared by Arab leaders that a Palestinian State would countenance *no Jewish inhabitants whatsoever*. This reflects what has become a totally apartheid policy nurtured by such statements as that of Mahmoud Abbas, chairman of the Palestinian Authority, who has declared: *"I will never allow a single Israeli to live among us on Palestinian land"*.[114] Not only is such a declaration in flagrant violation of this same international treaty (the Mandate) governing all the territory formerly known as Palestine—and perhaps most particularly that which was ultimately designated as the Jewish national home, west of the Jordan River, now challenged by the prospect of a yet further reduction of Israeli territory—but the Jews would once again become refugees from their own Land.

---

113 *Virtual Jerusalem*, http://www.virtualjerusalem.com/news.php?Itemid=4588; posted: 26 August 2011.
114 Mahmoud Abbas, speaking to Egyptian media on 28 July 2010. See also text accompanying note 94, *supra*.

10. THE ROLE OF THE UNITED NATIONS

Prior to the 2011 Annual Session of the United Nations General Assembly in New York, Palestinian Authority chairman Mahmoud Abbas announced his plan to formally request that a UN resolution be presented to the Security Council and assembled national delegations to "recognize" a unilaterally declared Palestinian State, with "East Jerusalem" as its capital, along with UN membership. The end result was that the Security Council, after extended consultations, was unable to reach a common position. Threats of a veto on the part of the United States and of abstentions on the part of Britain and France were based on grounds that recognition of a Palestinian state at this time would undermine the prospects for a bilaterally negotiated settlement (as called for in the Oslo Accords). Absent the needed support from these key representatives of the community of nations, the issue was not pressed to a vote—either in the Security Council or in the General Assembly—at the UN's 66th Session in 2011. The issue, however, is still very much alive.

It should be pointed out that, had there been or were there ever to be such "recognition" of the "Palestinians" as a political/statal entity, this would not, in and of itself, constitute the creation of a State of Palestine under international law, any more than the 1947 Resolution 181 (II) (the UN Partition Plan) created the State of Israel.[115]

Neither does membership in the United Nations *per se* create, confer or confirm statehood. UN membership requires nomination by the UN Security Council, with the unanimous support of the five Permanent Members (China, France, the Russian Federation, the United Kingdom and the United States). A contemporary example is that of Kosovo, which is recognized by at least seventy-five sovereign nations, yet its membership in the UN is precluded by the absence of the support of only one Permanent Member of the Security Council, namely, the Russian Federation.

According to the UN Charter, the General Assembly (GA) does not have the power to create legally binding decisions. It has only the power to recommend. UNGA resolutions are therefore not legally binding and the General Assembly lacks any and all competence to enact international law. In fact, the Charter does not authorize even the International Court of Justice (I.C.J.)—the principal judicial organ of the UN—to create, enact or amend international law.

---

115   See Part I, section 10 (esp. final para.) and Part II, section 1, *supra*.

According to one illustrious former president of the International Court, Professor Judge Schwebel:

> The General Assembly of the United Nations can only, in principle, issue "recommendations" which are not of a binding character, according to Article 10 of the Charter of the United Nations.[116]

The venerable Judges Sir Hersch Lauterpacht and Sir Gerald Fitzmaurice similarly confirmed the lack of "legislative effect" or "legal power to legislate or bind its members by way of recommendation".

Professor Arangio-Ruiz, who wrote what was considered "perhaps the most comprehensive" treatise ever compiled on the normative role of the UN General Assembly, went so far as to conclude that:

> [T]he General Assembly lacks legal authority either to "enact" or to "declare" or "determine" or "interpret" international law so as legally to bind states by such acts, whether these states be members of the United Nations or not, and whether these states voted for or against or abstained from the relevant vote or did not take part in it.[117]

At least on one point, then—that of the non-binding character of UNGA resolutions—there is no room for interpretation.

In the final analysis, there is categorically no practicable solution other than two legitimate governing entities that recognize and respect one another's rightful and legal existence, coming to the negotiating table and discussing all unresolved outstanding issues on permanent status, as per the relevant international legal commitments and binding instruments, with the aim of achieving a durable peace with secure and defensible borders.

---

116   See Eli E. Hertz, "ICJ—Bypassing the UN Security Council", Myth and Fact, 5 April 2011.

117   See *ibid.*

CONCLUSION

IT IS WIDELY assumed that the State of Israel was born as a result of UN Resolution 181 (the UN Partition Plan) of 1947. The truth is that the legal rights of the Jewish people and Israel as a nation find their foundations solidly embedded in international law well before the very existence of the United Nations, dating back to international legal instruments agreed by the Principal Allied Powers of World War I, meeting in San Remo in April of 1920 as a follow-up to the 1919 Paris Peace Conference.

It was at this place and time that the *historical* claim of the Jewish delegation to a "national home", as presented to the Supreme Council of the Principal Allied and Associated Powers in Paris, became *"essentially legal in character"*.[118] This legal character was codified in a binding international legal instrument in the form of the San Remo Resolution of April 1920, as reconfirmed and strengthened in July 1922 by the adoption of the Mandate for Palestine by the League of Nations.

Despite the fulfillment in May of 1948 of one of the Mandate's fundamental objectives, namely, the reconstitution of the Jewish national home, the Mandate's relevant provisions remain valid and legally binding to this day. Such provisions are, for example, applicable to the determination of the "core issues" to be negotiated between the two parties on the "permanent status" (or "final status") of Jerusalem and remaining disputed territory. Certain clauses regarding Jerusalem are even explicitly stated to be secured "in perpetuity".[119]

In sum, the conflict is not essentially a dispute over "borders" *per se*; that is not even really the issue, as demonstrated by the fact that national boundaries have gone so long undetermined. It is a dispute rather over *control* of *"disputed territory"*, in the near term, and permanent sovereignty over legitimate territorial jurisdictions, including the Old City of Jerusalem, in the long term. The sovereign jurisdiction rests with Israel, in the absence of some legally defensible cause for abrogating the Mandate for Palestine which contains no provisions

---

118 Gauthier, *supra* note 12, with reference to the classification of territorial claims elaborated by Professor Norman Hill.
119 See Mandate for Palestine, Appendix IV, Article 28.

for further carving up the territory designated in 1920/1922 by the Supreme Council of the Principal Allied Powers as the sole and unique national home for the Jewish people.

Appendix I

THE BALFOUR DECLARATION

Foreign Office,
November 2nd, 1917.

Dear Lord Rothschild,

I have much pleasure in conveying to you, on behalf of His Majesty's Government, the following declaration of sympathy with Jewish Zionist aspirations which has been submitted to, and approved by, the Cabinet

His Majesty's Government view with favour the establishment in Palestine of a national home for the Jewish people, and will use their best endeavours to facilitate the achievement of this object, it being clearly understood that nothing shall be done which may prejudice the civil and religious rights of existing non-Jewish communities in Palestine, or the rights and political status enjoyed by Jews in any other country"

I should be grateful if you would bring this declaration to the knowledge of the Zionist Federation.

Arthur James Balfour

Appendix II

ARTICLE 22
OF THE
COVENANT OF THE
LEAGUE OF NATIONS

ARTICLE 22

To those colonies and territories which as a consequence of the late war have ceased to be under the sovereignty of the States which formerly governed them and which are inhabited by peoples not yet able to stand by themselves under the strenuous conditions of the modern world, there should be applied the principle that the well-being and development of such peoples form a sacred trust of civilisation and that securities for the performance of this trust should be embodied in this Covenant.

The best method of giving practical effect to this principle is that the tutelage of such peoples should be entrusted to advanced nations who by reason of their resources, their experience or their geographical position can best undertake this responsibility, and who are willing to accept it, and that this tutelage should be exercised by them as Mandatories on behalf of the League.

The character of the mandate must differ according to the stage of the development of the people, the geographical situation of the territory, its economic conditions and other similar circumstances.

Certain communities formerly belonging to the Turkish Empire have reached a stage of development where their existence as independent nations can be provisionally recognized subject to the rendering of administrative advice and assistance by a Mandatory until such time as they are able to stand alone. The wishes of these communities must be a principal consideration in the selection of the Mandatory.

Other peoples, especially those of Central Africa, are at such a stage that the Mandatory must be responsible for the administration of the territory under conditions which will guarantee freedom of conscience and religion, subject only to the maintenance of public order and morals, the prohibition of abuses such as the slave trade, the arms traffic and the liquor traffic, and the prevention of the establishment of fortifications or military and naval bases and of military training of the natives for other than police purposes and the defence of territory, and will also secure equal opportunities for the trade and commerce of other Members of the League.

There are territories, such as South-West Africa and certain of the South Pacific Islands, which, owing to the sparseness of their population, or their small size, or their remoteness from the centres of civilisation, or their geographical contiguity to the territory of the Mandatory, and other circumstances, can be best administered under the laws of the Mandatory as integral portions of its territory, subject to the safeguards above mentioned in the interests of the indigenous population.

In every case of mandate, the Mandatory shall render to the Council an annual report in reference to the territory committed to its charge.

The degree of authority, control, or administration to be exercised by the Mandatory shall, if not previously agreed upon by the Members of the League, be explicitly defined in each case by the Council.

A permanent Commission shall be constituted to receive and examine the annual reports of the Mandatories and to advise the Council on all matters relating to the observance of the mandates.

Appendix III

THE SAN REMO RESOLUTION

It was agreed—

(a) To accept the terms of the Mandates Article as given below with reference to Palestine, on the understanding that there was inserted in the proces-verbal an undertaking by the Mandatory Power that this would not involve the surrender of the rights hitherto enjoyed by the non-Jewish communities in Palestine; this undertaking not to refer to the question of the religious protectorate of France, which had been settled earlier in the previous afternoon by the undertaking given by the French Government that they recognized this protectorate as being at an end.

(b) that the terms of the Mandates Article should be as follows:

The High Contracting Parties agree that Syria and Mesopotamia shall, in accordance with the fourth paragraph of Article 22, Part I (Covenant of the League of Nations), be provisionally recognized as independent States, subject to the rendering of administrative advice and assistance by a mandatory until such time as they are able to stand alone. The boundaries of the said States will be determined, and the selection of the Mandatories made, by the Principal Allied Powers.

The High Contracting Parties agree to entrust, by application of the provisions of Article 22, the administration of Palestine, within such boundaries as may be determined by the Principal Allied Powers, to a Mandatory, to be selected by the said Powers. The Mandatory will be responsible for putting into effect the declaration originally made on November 8, 1917, by the British

Government, and adopted by the other Allied Powers, in favour of the establishment in Palestine of a national home for the Jewish people, it being clearly understood that nothing shall be done which may prejudice the civil and religious rights of existing non-Jewish communities in Palestine, or the rights and political status enjoyed by Jews in any other country.

La Puissance mandataire s'engage à nommer dans le plus bref délai une commission spéciale pour étudier toute question et toute réclamation concernant les différentes communautés religieuses et en établir le règlement. Il sera tenu compte dans la composition de cette commission des intérêts religieux en jeu. Le président de la commission sera nommé par le Conseil de la Société des Nations.

The terms of the mandates in respect of the above territories will be formulated by the Principal Allied Powers and submitted to the Council of the League of Nations for approval.

Turkey hereby undertakes, in accordance with the provisions of Article [132 of the Treaty of Sèvres] to accept any decisions which may be taken in this connection.

(c) Les mandataires choisis par les principales Puissances alliées sont: la France pour la Syrie, et la Grand-Bretagne pour la Mésopotamie et la Palestine.

In reference to the above decision the Supreme Council took note of the following reservation of the Italian Delegation:

La Délégation italienne en considération des grands intérêts économiques que l'Italie en tant que puissance exclusivement méditerranéenne possède en Asie Mineure, réserve son approbation à la présente résolution, jusqu'au règlement des intérêts italiens en Turquie d'Asie.

Appendix IV

THE MANDATE FOR PALESTINE

THE COUNCIL OF THE LEAGUE OF NATIONS

Whereas the Principal Allied Powers have agreed, for the purpose of giving effect to the provisions of Article 22 of the Covenant of the League of Nations, to entrust to a Mandatory selected by the said Powers the administration of the territory of Palestine, which formerly belonged to the Turkish Empire, within such boundaries as may be fixed by them; and

Whereas the Principal Allied Powers have also agreed that the Mandatory should be responsible for putting into effect the declaration originally made on November 2nd, 1917, by the Government of His Britannic Majesty, and adopted by the said Powers, in favour of the establishment in Palestine of a national home for the Jewish people, it being clearly understood that nothing should be done which might prejudice the civil and religious rights of existing non-Jewish communities in Palestine, or the rights and political status enjoyed by Jews in any other country ; and

Whereas recognition has thereby been given to the historical connection of the Jewish people with Palestine and to the grounds for reconstituting their national home in that country; and

Whereas the Principal Allied Powers have selected His Britannic Majesty as the Mandatory for Palestine; and

Whereas the mandate in respect of Palestine has been formulated in the following terms and submitted to the Council of the League for approval; and

Whereas His Britannic Majesty has accepted the mandate in respect of Palestine and undertaken to exercise it on behalf of the League of Nations in conformity with the following provisions; and

Whereas by the afore-mentioned Article 22 (paragraph 8), it is provided that the degree of authority, control or administration to be exercised by the Mandatory, not having been previously agreed upon by the Members of the League, shall be explicitly defined by the Council of the League of Nations;

Confirming the said mandate, defines its terms as follows:

Article 1.

The Mandatory shall have full powers of legislation and of administration, save as they may be limited by the terms of this mandate.

Article 2.

The Mandatory shall be responsible for placing the country under such political, administrative and economic conditions as will secure the establishment of the Jewish national home, as laid down in the preamble, and the development of self -governing institutions, and also for safeguarding the civil and religious rights of all the inhabitants of Palestine, irrespective of race and religion.

Article 3.

The Mandatory shall, so far as circumstances permit, encourage local autonomy.

Article 4.

An appropriate Jewish agency shall be recognised as a public body for the purpose of advising and co-operating with the Administration of Palestine in such economic, social and other matters as may affect the establishment of the Jewish national home and the interests of the Jewish population in Palestine, and, subject always to the control of the Administration, to assist and take part in the development of the country.

The Zionist organisation, so long as its organisation and constitution are in the opinion of the Mandatory appropriate, shall be recognised as such agency. It shall take steps in consultation with His Britannic Majesty's Government to secure the cooperation of all Jews who are willing to assist in the establishment of the Jewish national home.

Article 5.

The Mandatory shall be responsible for seeing that no Palestine territory shall be ceded or leased to, or in any way placed under the control of, the Government of any foreign Power.

Article 6.

The Administration of Palestine, while ensuring that the rights and position of other sections of the population are not prejudiced, shall facilitate Jewish immigration under suitable conditions and shall encourage, in co-operation with the Jewish agency. referred to in Article 4, close settlement by Jews, on the land, including State lands and waste lands not required for public purposes.

Article 7.

The Administration of Palestine shall be responsible for enacting a nationality law. There shall be included in this law provisions framed so as to facilitate the acquisition of Palestinian citizenship by Jews who take up their permanent residence in Palestine.

Article 8.

The privileges and immunities of foreigners, including the benefits of consular jurisdiction and protection as formerly enjoyed by Capitulation or usage in the Ottoman Empire, shall not be applicable in Palestine.

Unless the Powers whose nationals enjoyed the afore-mentioned privileges and immunities on August 1st, 1914, shall have previously renounced the right to their re-establishment, or shall have agreed to their non-application for a specified period, these privileges and immunities shall, at the expiration of the mandate, be immediately re-established in their entirety or with such modifications as may have been agreed upon between the Powers concerned.

Article 9.

The Mandatory shall be responsible for seeing that the judicial system established in Palestine shall assure to foreigners, as well as to natives, a complete guarantee of their rights.

Respect for the personal status of the various peoples and communities and for their religious interests shall be fully guaranteed. In particular, the control and administration of Wakfs shall be exercised in accordance with religious law and the dispositions of the founders.

Article 10.

Pending the making of special extradition agreements relating to Palestine, the extradition treaties in force between the Mandatory and other foreign Powers shall apply to Palestine.

Article 11.

The Administration of Palestine shall take all necessary measures to safeguard the interests of the community in connection with the development of the country, and, subject to any international obligations accepted by the Mandatory, shall have full power to provide for public ownership or control of any of the natural resources of the country or of the public works, services and utilities established or to be established therein. It shall introduce a land system appropriate to the needs of the country, having regard, among other things, to the desirability of promoting the close settlement and intensive cultivation of the land.

The Administration may arrange with the Jewish agency mentioned in Article 4 to construct or operate, upon fair and equitable terms, any public works, services and utilities, and to develop any of the natural resources of the country, in so far as these matters are not directly undertaken by the Administration. Any such arrangements shall provide that no profits distributed by such agency, directly or indirectly, shall exceed a reasonable rate of interest on the capital, and any further profits shall be utilised by it for the benefit of the country in a manner approved by the Administration.

Article 12.

The Mandatory shall be entrusted with the control of the foreign relations of Palestine and the right to issue exequaturs to consuls appointed by foreign Powers. He shall also be entitled to afford diplomatic and consular protection to citizens of Palestine when outside its territorial limits.

Article 13.

All responsibility in connection with the Holy Places and religious buildings or sites in Palestine, including that of preserving existing rights and of securing free access to the Holy Places, religious buildings and sites and the free exercise of worship, while ensuring the requirements of public order and decorum, is assumed by the Mandatory, who shall be responsible solely to the League of Nations. in all matters connected herewith, provided that nothing in this article shall prevent the Mandatory from entering into such arrangements as he may deem reasonable with the Administration for the purpose of carrying the provisions of this article into effect; and provided also that nothing in this mandate shall be construed as conferring upon the Mandatory authority to interfere with the fabric or the management of purely Moslem sacred shrines, the immunities of which are guaranteed.

Article 14.

A special Commission shall be appointed by the Mandatory to study, define and determine the rights and claims in connection with the Holy Places and the rights and claims relating to the different religious communities in Palestine.

The method of nomination, the composition and the functions of this Commission shall be submitted to the Council of the League for its approval, and the Commission shall not be appointed or enter upon its functions without the approval of the Council.

Article 15.

The Mandatory shall see that complete freedom of conscience and the free exercise of all forms of worship, subject only to the maintenance of public order and morals, are ensured to all. No discrimination of any kind shall be made between the inhabitants of Palestine on the ground of race, religion or language. No person shall be excluded from Palestine on the sole ground of his religious belief.

The right of each community to maintain its own schools for the education of its own members in its own language, while conforming to such educational requirements of a general nature as the Administration may impose, shall not be denied or impaired.

Article 16.

The Mandatory shall be responsible for exercising such supervision over religious or eleemosynary bodies of all faiths in Palestine as may be required for the maintenance of public order and good government. Subject to such supervision, no measures shall be taken in Palestine to obstruct or interfere with the enterprise of such bodies or to discriminate against any representative or member of them on the ground of his religion or nationality.

Article 17.

The Administration of Palestine may organise on a voluntary basis the forces necessary for the preservation of peace and order, and also for the defence of the country, subject, however, to the supervision of the Mandatory, but shall not use them for purposes other than those above specified save with the consent of the Mandatory, Except for such purposes, no military, naval or air forces shall be raised or maintained by the Administration of Palestine.

Nothing in this article shall preclude the Administration of Palestine from contributing to the cost of the maintenance of the forces of the Mandatory in Palestine.

The Mandatory shall be entitled at all times to use the roads, railways and ports of Palestine for the movement of armed forces and the carriage of fuel and supplies.

Article 18.

The Mandatory shall see that there is no discrimination in Palestine against the nationals of any State Member of the League of Nations (including companies incorporated under its laws) as compared with those of the Mandatory or of any foreign State in matters concerning taxation, commerce or navigation, the exercise of industries or professions, or in the treatment of merchant vessels or civil aircraft. Similarly, there shall be no discrimination in

Palestine against goods originating in or destined for any of the said States, and there shall be freedom of transit under equitable conditions across the mandated area.

Subject as aforesaid and to the other provisions of this mandate, the Administration of Palestine may, on the advice of the Mandatory, impose such taxes and customs duties as it may consider necessary, and take such steps as it may think best to promote the development of the natural resources of the country and to safeguard the interests of the population. It may also, on the advice of the Mandatory, conclude a special customs agreement with any State the territory of which in 1914 was wholly included in Asiatic Turkey or Arabia.

Article 19.

The Mandatory shall adhere on behalf of the Administration of Palestine to any general international conventions already existing, or which may be concluded hereafter with the approval of the League of Nations, respecting the slave traffic, the traffic in arms and ammunition, or the traffic in drugs, or relating to commercial equality, freedom of transit and navigation, aerial navigation and postal, telegraphic and wireless communication or literary, artistic or industrial property.

Article 20.

The Mandatory shall co-operate on behalf of the Administration of Palestine, so far as religious, social and other conditions may permit, in the execution of any common policy adopted by the League of Nations for preventing and combating disease, including diseases of plants and animals.

Article 21.

The Mandatory shall secure the enactment within twelve months from this date, and shall ensure the execution of a Law of Antiquities based on the following rules. This law shall ensure equality of treatment in the matter of excavations and archaeological research to the nations of all States Members of the League of Nations.

(1) 'Antiquity' means any construction or any product of human activity earlier than the year A.D. 1700.

(2) The law for the protection of antiquities shall proceed by encouragement rather than by threat.

Any person who, having discovered an antiquity without being furnished with the authorisation referred to in paragraph 5, reports the same to an official of the competent Department, shall be rewarded according to the value of the discovery.

(3) No antiquity may be disposed of except to the competent Department, unless this Department renounces the acquisition of any such antiquity.

No antiquity may leave the country without an export licence from the said Department.

(4) Any person who maliciously or negligently destroys or damages an antiquity shall be liable to a penalty to be fixed.

(5) No clearing of ground or digging with the object of finding antiquities shall be permitted, under penalty of fine, except to persons authorised by the competent Department.

(6) Equitable terms shall be fixed for expropriation, temporary or permanent, of lands which might be of historical or archaeological interest.

(7) Authorisation to excavate shall only be granted to persons who show sufficient guarantees of archaeological experience. The Administration of Palestine shall not, in granting these authorisations, act in such a way as to exclude scholars of any nation without good grounds.

(8) The proceeds of excavations may be divided between the excavator and the competent Department in a proportion fixed by that Department. If division seems impossible for scientific reasons, the excavator shall receive a fair indemnity in lieu of a part of the find.

Article 22.

English, Arabic and Hebrew shall be the official languages of Palestine. Any statement or inscription in Arabic on stamps or money in Palestine shall be repeated in Hebrew, and any statement or inscription in Hebrew shall be repeated in Arabic.

Article 23.

The Administration of Palestine shall recognise the holy days of the respective communities in Palestine as legal days of rest for the members of such communities.

Article 24.

The Mandatory shall make to the Council of the League of Nations an annual report to the satisfaction of the Council as to the measures taken during the year to carry out the provisions of the mandate. Copies of all laws and regulations promulgated or issued during the year shall be communicated with the report.

Article 25.

In the territories lying between the Jordan and the eastern boundary of Palestine as ultimately determined, the Mandatory shall be entitled, with the consent of the Council of the League of Nations, to postpone or withhold application of such provisions of this mandate as he may consider inapplicable to the existing local conditions, and to make such provision for the administration of the territories as he may consider suitable to those conditions, provided that no action shall be taken which is inconsistent with the provisions of Articles 15, 16 and 18.

Article 26.

The Mandatory agrees that, if any dispute whatever should arise between the Mandatory and another Member of the League of Nations relating to the interpretation or the application of the provisions of the mandate, such dispute, if it cannot be settled by negotiation, shall be submitted to the Permanent Court of International Justice provided for by Article 14 of the Covenant of the League of Nations.

Article 27.

The consent of the Council of the League of Nations is required for any modification of the terms of this mandate.

Article 28.

In the event of the termination of the mandate hereby conferred upon the Mandatory, the Council of the League of Nations shall make such arrangements as may be deemed necessary for safeguarding in perpetuity, under guarantee of the League, the rights secured by Articles 13 and 14, and shall use its influence for securing, under the guarantee of the League, that the Government of Palestine will fully honour the financial obligations legitimately incurred by the Administration of Palestine during the period of the mandate, including the rights of public servants ,to pensions or gratuities.

The present instrument shall be deposited in original in the archives of the League of Nations and certified copies shall be forwarded by the Secretary-General of the League of Nations to all Members of the League.

Appendix V

GEOGRAPHICAL MAPS OF THE TERRITORY OF PALESTINE[120]

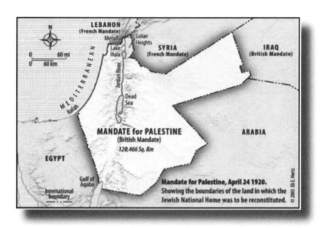

Mandate for Palestine, April 24 1920.
Showing the boundaries of the land in which the Jewish National Home was to be reconstituted.

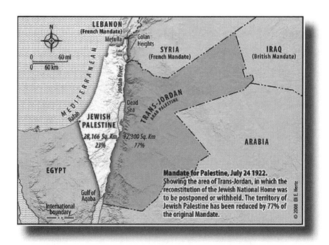

Mandate for Palestine, July 24 1922.
Showing the area of Trans-Jordan, in which the reconstitution of the Jewish National Home was to be postponed or withheld. The territory of Jewish Palestine has been reduced by 77% of the original Mandate.

120   Source: www.mythandfacts.org.

ABSTRACT

See French, German and Italian translations of Abstract herein, while noting that only the original English text is authoritative.

PART I: FOUNDATIONS OF THE INTERNATIONAL LEGAL RIGHTS OF THE JEWISH PEOPLE AND THE STATE OF ISRAEL

I N INTERNATIONAL LAW, as in all law, there are always two sides to a question. If this were not the case, there would be little need for legal solutions. Moreover, both parties in any conflict believe the right is on their side, or at least that they have means to prove this to be so. Accordingly, no law is ever created in a vacuum; a law is created when a serious enough need arises.

In 1917, owing to the events of World War I, a serious need was identified and a voice was raised. The need was that of the Jewish people, dispersed across the earth for some two thousand years, to have a national home. The voice was that of Lord Balfour, speaking on behalf of the British War Cabinet in defense of the Jewish people worldwide. This compelling need found official expression in the Balfour Declaration of 1917.

The *Balfour Declaration* was a *political* statement with no legal authority; moreover, it was *not international*. Nonetheless it was a major turning point in the history of the dispersed Jewish people, giving them a future hope of eventually fulfilling their never dying longing for their ancient Holy Land. What it accomplished was to raise the profile, internationally, of the need of a stateless people to have a "national home" to which they could return. Of monumental significance was the official recognition of the all-important *historic, religious* and *cultural* links of the Jews to the land of their forefathers, the land that had come to be known under the Greeks and Romans as "Palestine".

Because the cause was just and the concept justified, there needed to be a way to elevate the content of this Declaration to the level of international law. Accordingly, the matter was taken up by the Supreme Council of the Principal Allied and Associated Powers (Britain, France, Italy, Japan and the United States) at the Paris Peace Conference in 1919. The issue became more complex as submissions for territorial claims were presented by both Arab and Jewish delegations, as the old Ottoman Empire was being apportioned out to the victorious Powers; thus the matter was not able to be settled within the time frame of the Paris Conference.

What did happen at the Paris Conference that factored into the progression of events we are considering here was the establishment of the *League of Nations* which, in Article 22 of its Covenant, provided for the setting up of a mandate system as a trust for the Old Ottoman territories.

The next important milestone on the road to international legal status and a Jewish national home was the *San Remo Conference*, held at Villa Devachan in San Remo, Italy, from 18 to 26 April 1920. This was an 'extension' of the Paris Peace Conference of 1919 for the purpose of dealing with some of these outstanding issues. The aim of the four (out of five) members of the Supreme Council of the Principal Allied and Associated Powers that met in San Remo (the United States being present as observer only, owing to the new non-interventionist policy of President Woodrow Wilson), was to consider the earlier submissions of the claimants, to deliberate and to make decisions on the legal recognition of each claim. The outcome, relying on Article 22 of the Covenant of the League of Nations, was the setting up of three mandates, one over Syria and Lebanon (later separated into two mandates), one over Mesopotamia (Iraq), and one over Palestine. The *Mandate for Palestine* was entrusted to Great Britain, as a "sacred trust of civilization" in respect of "the establishment in Palestine of a National Home for the Jewish people". This was a binding resolution with all the force of international law.

In two out of the original three Mandates, it was recognized that the indigenous people had the capacity to govern themselves, with the Mandatory Power merely assisting in the establishment of the institutions of government, where necessary. This was not true of Palestine, as Palestine was, under the Mandate, to become a homeland ("national home") for the Jewish people. Although the Jewish people were part of the indigenous population of Palestine, the majority of them at that time were not living in the Land. The Mandate for Palestine was thus quite different from the others and set out how the Land was to be settled by Jews in preparation for their forming a viable nation in the territory then known as "Palestine". The *unique* obligations of the Mandatory to the Jewish people in respect of the establishment of their national home in Palestine thus gave a *sui generis* (unique, one of a kind) character to the Mandate for Palestine. The boundaries of the "Palestine" referred to in the claimants' submissions included territories *west and east* of the Jordan River. The submissions of the Jewish claimants specified that the ultimate purpose of the mandate would be the "creation of an autonomous commonwealth", provided "that nothing must be done that might prejudice the civil and religious rights of the non-Jewish communities at present established in Palestine". The resulting Mandate for Palestine, approved by the Council of the League of Nations in July 1922, was an international treaty and, as such, was legally binding.

The decision made in San Remo was a watershed moment in the history of the Jewish people who had been a people without a home for some two thousand years. From the perspective of Chaim Weizmann, president of the newly formed Zionist Organization and later to become the first President of the State of Israel, "recognition of our rights in Palestine is embodied in the treaty with Turkey, and has become part of international law. This is the most momentous political event in the whole history of our movement, and it is, perhaps, no exaggeration to say in the whole history of our people since the Exile." To the Zionist Organization of America, the San Remo Resolution "crowns the British [Balfour] declaration by enacting it as part of the law of nations of the world."

The policy to be given effect in the Mandate for Palestine was consistent with the Balfour Declaration, in significantly recognizing the *historic, cultural* and *religious* ties of the Jewish people to the Holy Land, and even stronger than the Declaration through the insertion of the fundamental principle that Palestine should be *reconstituted* as the national home of the Jewish people. It is particularly relevant to underline the inclusion in the terms of the Mandate (through Article 2) of the fundamental principle set out in the Preamble of this international agreement that "recognition has thereby been given to the historical connection of the Jewish people with Palestine and to the grounds for *reconstituting* their national home in that country".

The *primary objective of the Mandate* was to provide *a national home for the Jewish people*—including Jewish people dispersed *worldwide*—in their ancestral home. The Arab people, who already exercised sovereignty in a number of States, were guaranteed protection of their civil and religious rights under the Mandate as long as they wished to remain, even after the State of Israel was ultimately formed in 1948. Moreover, Trans-Jordan was meanwhile added as a territory under Arab sovereignty, *carved out of the very mandated territory at issue*, by the British, prior to the actual signing of the Mandate in 1922 (see below).

When the Council of the League of Nations approved the Mandate for Palestine in July 1922, it became binding on all 51 Members of the League. This act of the League enabled the ultimate realization of the long cherished dream of the *restoration* of the Jewish people to *their ancient land* and *validated the existence of historical facts and events linking the Jewish people to Palestine*. For the Supreme Council of the Principal Allied Powers, and for the Council of the League of Nations, these *historical facts* were considered to be *accepted and established*. In the words of Neville Barbour, "*In 1922, international sanction was given to the Balfour Declaration by the issue of the Palestine Mandate*".

The rights granted to the Jewish people in the Mandate for Palestine were to be given effect in *all of Palestine*. It thus follows that the *legal rights* of the claimants to sovereignty over the *Old City of Jerusalem* similarly derive from the decisions of the Supreme Council of the Principal Allied Powers in San Remo and from the terms of the Mandate for Palestine approved by the Council of the League of Nations.

In March 1921, in Cairo, Great Britain decided to partition the mandated territory of Palestine, for international political reasons of its own. Article 25 of the Mandate gave the Mandatory Power permission to postpone or withhold most of the terms of the Mandate in the area of land east of the Jordan River ("Trans-Jordan"). Great Britain, as Mandatory Power, exercised that right.

For former UN Ambassador, Professor Yehuda Zvi Blum, *the rights vested in the Arab people of Palestine with respect to the principle of self-determination were fulfilled as a result of this initial partition of Palestine approved by the Council of the League of Nations in 1922. According to Professor Blum: "The Palestinian Arabs have long enjoyed self-determination in their own state – the Palestinian Arab State of Jordan"*. (Worth mentioning here, in a letter apparently written on 17 January 1921 to Churchill's Private Secretary, Col. T.E. Lawrence ("of Arabia") had reported that, in return for Arab sovereignty in Iraq, Trans-Jordan and Syria, King Hussein's eldest son, Emir Feisal—a man said by Lawrence to be known for keeping his word—had "*agreed to abandon all claims of his father to Palestine*".)

After this partition, Churchill—British Colonial Secretary at the time—immediately reaffirmed the commitment of Great Britain to give effect to the policies of the Balfour Declaration in *all the other parts of the territory* covered by the Mandate for Palestine west of the Jordan River. *This pledge included the area of Jerusalem and its Old City.* In Churchill's own words: "It is manifestly right that the Jews who are scattered all over the world should have a national centre and a national home where some of them may be reunited. And where else could that be but in the land of Palestine, with which for more than three thousand years they have been intimately and profoundly associated?"

Thus, in a word, *the primary foundations in international law for the "legal" claim based on "historic rights" or "historic title" of the Jewish people in respect of Palestine are the San Remo decisions of April 1920, the Mandate for Palestine of July 1922*, approved by the Council of the League of Nations and bearing the signatures of those same Principal Allied Powers but rendering it an international treaty binding on all Member States, *and the Covenant of the League of Nations itself (Art. 22).*

PART II: THE QUESTION OF A UNILATERAL DECLARATION OF A STATE OF PALESTINE

Many years passed from the adoption of the Mandate in 1922 to the creation of the State of Israel in 1948. An event that precipitated Israeli statehood was the vote by the UN General Assembly in 1947 for the partition of Palestine (Resolution 181 (II)), recommending the setting up of a Jewish and an Arab State in that territory. While UNGA resolutions are no more than recommendatory, with no legally binding force, the Jews accepted the partition plan, whereas the Arabs rejected it. The UK terminated its role as Mandatory Power and pulled out of the territory on 14 May 1948. On that date, to take effect at midnight, the Jews declared the State of Israel.

The following day, the armies of five surrounding Arab nations attacked the new Jewish State (Israeli War of Independence). The

Arabs unexpectedly met defeat, though Jordan illegally annexed Judea and Samaria. Israel regained control over its mandated territory in a war of self-defence, the Six-Day War, in 1967.

Despite these intervening events that have since influenced its ongoing relevance, not least of which being the fulfillment of its primary purpose, the creation of a Jewish State, certain fundamental aspects of the Mandate remain valid and legally binding and are highly relevant for the determination of the "core issues" to be negotiated between the two parties on the "permanent status" (or "final status") of Jerusalem and the "West Bank".

In order to get the proper perspective in considering the international legal framework surrounding the question of a unilaterally declared Palestinian State with the eastern part of Jerusalem as its capital, we may need to go beyond the law, *per se*, to consider the impact of public opinion on the formulation of both customary and codified international law. Accordingly, attention should be drawn to the degree to which equitable resolutions to the "core issues" of today's Israeli / Arab Palestinian conflict can be exacerbated by linguistic hyperbole, factual distortion or pure political manoeuvring and calculated rhetoric. Some of this rhetoric has a critical need to be subjected to the light of legal terminology and precision. Otherwise it can easily lead to gross distortions of truth, which can even result in ill-advised international legal responses.

Take for example, the *"Palestinian" identity*. At the time of the San Remo decision and the resulting Mandate for Palestine, the territory then known as "Palestine" was designated expressly for the *"reconstitution"* of the "national home" of the Jewish people *only*. While care was taken to protect the rights of Arab inhabitants, the Jews alone were a people without a country. Indeed, this was the very purpose of the Mandate for Palestine and its predecessor the Balfour Declaration. At the time of the Mandate, it would have been more accurate to refer to "Palestinian Jews" and "Palestinian Arabs" (along with various other non-Jewish inhabitants). But because of the creation of the State of Israel, the Palestinian Jews retained their ancient name of "Israelis" while the non-Jews (mainly but not all Arabs) appropriated the name "Palestinians", with the result that they are often erroneously viewed as being the rightful inhabitants of the Land. In actual fact, the Land called "Palestine" covers territory that the Jews have called the "Holy Land" well before the name "Palestine" was first used by the Greeks and Romans. The truth is that the territory known as "Palestine" has never—either since this name was applied or before—been an Arab nation or been designated to be an Arab nation. But this nomenclature carries great psychological impact with the inference that it is the former Arab inhabitants of Palestine that are the *true* "Palestinians" and that they *alone* belong in "Palestine".

As regards the *refugee question*, the legal definition of "refugee" is "a person who flees or is expelled from a country, esp[ecially] because of persecution, and seeks haven in another country" (*Black's Law Dictionary*). The present plight of all those living in refugee camps is truly pitiable and rightfully arouses the compassion of the world; but most Palestinians identified as "refugees" are well over a generation away from the events that caused the foregoing generation to flee. Vast Arab lands were accorded statehood generations ago and could easily accommodate all these most unfortunate "refugees" who have been made a spectacle of for six decades instead of being integrated as productive members of society among their own people. *In addition* to the other San Remo mandated territories that gained statehood before Israel, and could well have absorbed their Arab brothers, Trans-Jordan was partitioned off *specially* for the Palestinian Arabs in the territory originally designated for the Jewish national home. *This already furnished a legitimate 'new State' for the Arabs within the territory of "Palestine".* International law has never had to grapple with the question of the 'inheritance' of refugee status, such a situation being unique in human history.

Concerning the *"1967 lines"*, as a point of reference for a potential new Palestinian State, there is constant mention of withdrawal to the "1967 *borders*". Firstly, this terminology is legally incorrect. The word "borders" is generally used in international law to mean "national boundaries", which the 1967 "lines" most decidedly are not. The definition of a "border" under international law is "a boundary between one nation (or a political subdivision [of that nation]) and another" (*Black's Law Dictionary*). No such national boundaries have ever been established for the reborn State of Israel. The 1967 "lines" are purely *military* no-cross lines ("armistice demarcation lines"), from Israel's 1948 War of Independence. These "lines" have been *expressly* repeated in *numerous* 1949 Israeli-Palestinian armistice agreements to neither represent national borders nor prejudice the future bilateral negotiation of same. These 1949 armistice lines remained valid until the outbreak of the 1967 Six-Day War. Linking them with the 1967 war – where lost territory was recovered by the Israel Defense Forces, under attack – by calling them "1967 borders" instead of 1949 armistice lines, fosters the erroneous notion that these are ill-gotten "borders", thus highly prejudicing the issue and its outcome. Eugene Rostow, U.S. Undersecretary of State for Political Affairs in 1967 and one of the drafters of the 1967 UN Security Council *Resolution 242* on "safe and secure" borders, stated in 1990 that it and subsequent Security Council Resolution 338 "...rest on two principles, Israel may administer the territory until its Arab neighbors make peace; and when peace is made, Israel should withdraw to 'secure and recognized borders,' which need not be the same as the Armistice Demarcation Lines of 1949". In a word, the 1967 lines are *not* "borders" at all, and this word should not be used to create and perpetuate the impression that Israel has illegally transgressed the borders of another state, when this is clearly not the case.

Similarly, with regard to the *disputed territories*, the widespread use of the words "occupied territory" rather than "disputed territory" (which in fact it is) has a major psychological impact that can result in real and even legal ramifications. Furthermore, this language and what it tends to connote ("belligerent occupation") totally ignores the international treaty language of *"reconstituted"*, as contained in the Mandate for Palestine. *Reconstituted* territory precludes "belligerent occupation", even if permanent national borders have yet to be negotiated. A state cannot, by definition, be a "belligerent occupying power" in a territory that is being "reconstituted" in its name, according to the provisions of a legally binding instrument of international law. "[O]ccupation occurs when a belligerent state invades the territory of another state with the intention of holding the territory at least temporarily" (West's Encyclopedia of American Law). The territory that Israel reclaimed in 1967 was never rightfully "the territory of another state", nor did Israel obtain it by war of aggression. Indeed, it was territory that had been specifically designated for a *Jewish* national home, under the legally binding Mandate for Palestine in 1922.

A close corollary is the question of *settlements*. The sensitivities surrounding this question are exacerbated by the very fact that the legality/illegality of such settlements is based on factors that may not follow prescribed international law norms but rather are complicated by the unique nature of the Israeli case. For example, while it is often claimed that such settlements violate Article 49 of the Geneva Convention (IV), the inclusion of this article in the Convention had a different purpose altogether than to govern circumstances such as those existing in present-day Israel. The drafters' intent was that of

protecting vulnerable civilians in times of armed conflict by creating
an international legal instrument that would declare as unlawful
all *coerced deportation* such as that suffered by over forty million
Germans, Soviets, Poles, Ukrainians, Hungarians and others, immediately after the Second World War. In the case of Israel, under international law as embodied in the Mandate for Palestine, Jews were
permitted and even *encouraged* to settle in *every part* of Palestine;
they were *not* deported or forcibly transferred. Accordingly, calling
the "East Jerusalem", Judea and Samaria Israeli settlements "illegal"
is not an apt application of the Fourth Geneva Convention.

The *question of Jerusalem* may be the most volatile of all. Owing
to the sacredness of this city to so many, it has become evident that
the positions of Israel and the Palestinians regarding the Old City
are virtually irreconcilable. Evidence of this is the fact that it was
not named in the Framework for Peace in the Middle East, agreed in
the 1978 Camp David Accords between Israel and Egypt. In the latter
case, Jerusalem was indeed on the agenda, but was left out of the
actual Accords, owing to the inability of the two parties to resolve
their fundamental differences on the highly loaded issue. The failure
of the Camp David Summit of July 2000 again underlined the significance of the question of Jerusalem and its Old City.

Coming to the *role of the United Nations* in the current debate, it
must be recalled that, according to the UN Charter, the UN General
Assembly does not have the power to create legally binding decisions. General Assembly Resolutions have only the power to recommend, with no legally binding force. Therefore, were there to be a
Resolution "recognizing" the "Arab Palestinians" as a political/state
entity, this would not, in and of itself, constitute the creation of a
State of Palestine under international law, any more than the 1947
Resolution 181 (II) (the UN Partition Plan) created the State of Israel.

Moreover there have been commitments on both sides to *"permanent status"* negotiations. The PLO leadership pledged in 1993 to
commit virtually *all* the important issues of "permanent status" to
resolution by *negotiations only*. Under the 1995 Interim Agreement
(Oslo II), the parties undertook *not to act unilaterally* to alter the
status of the territories prior to the results of permanent status negotiations. It was clearly stipulated and agreed that: "... *neither side
shall initiate or take any step* that will *change the status* of the West
Bank and the Gaza strip pending the outcome of *the permanent
status negotiations*" (emphasis added).

A unilaterally declared Palestinian State would therefore be in breach of commitments embodied in an international legal instrument as well in publicly declared and published official statements and documents.

In sum, the conflict is not a traditional conflict over *borders*—that is not even really the issue, as demonstrated by the fact that national boundaries have gone so long undetermined. It is a conflict over historic rights and the internationally recognized need of a unified 'people' to have a place (and territorial space) to come 'home' to after some two thousand years of 'statelessness' and separation from the Land of their fathers—the *only* place that they call "holy" and the *only* Land they have ever called "home".

RÉSUMÉ

Traduction. Seule la version originale en anglais fait foi.

PARTIE I : LES FONDATIONS DES DROITS JURIDIQUES INTERNATIONAUX DU PEUPLE JUIF ET DE L'ETAT D'ISRAËL

En droit international, comme dans toute loi, il y a toujours deux côtés dans un litige. Sans cela, les solutions juridiques ne seraient pas vraiment nécessaires. De surcroît, les deux parties d'un conflit pensent toutes les deux que le droit est de leur côté ou tout au moins qu'elles ont les moyens de prouver qu'il en est ainsi. Par conséquent, aucune loi n'est jamais créée sans aucune raison, elle l'est lorsqu'un besoin suffisamment sérieux se manifeste.

En 1917, une voix se fit entendre car un besoin sérieux fut identifié suite aux évènements de la Première Guerre mondiale. Le peuple juif, dispersé de par le monde depuis environ 2000 ans, avait besoin d'un foyer national. Cette voix fut celle de Lord Balfour qui s'exprima au nom du cabinet de guerre britannique (British War Cabinet) pour défendre le peuple juif du monde entier. Cette nécessité impérieuse trouva son expression officielle dans la Déclaration Balfour de 1917.

La Déclaration Balfour fut une déclaration politique sans aucune autorité légale, ni portée internationale. Néanmoins, elle marqua un tournant décisif dans l'histoire du peuple juif dispersé car elle leur donna l'espoir que dans l'avenir leur désir inlassable de retourner sur leur ancienne Terre Sainte serait peut-être un jour satisfait. Elle permit de dresser le profil, au niveau international, du besoin d'un peuple apatride d'avoir un « foyer national » dans lequel il pourrait retourner. La reconnaissance officielle des liens historiques, religieux et culturels des Juifs à la terre de leurs ancêtres, qui au temps des Grecs et des Romains était appelée « Palestine », fut d'une importance majeure. Etant donné que la cause était juste et que le concept était justifié, un moyen devait être trouvé afin d'élever le contenu de cette déclaration au niveau du droit international. Par conséquent, en 1919, l'affaire fut saisie par le Conseil suprême des principales puissances alliées et associées (Grande-Bretagne, France, Italie, Japon et les Etats-Unis) lors de la Conférence de paix de Paris. La question devint plus complexe d'une part, parce que les soumissions des revendications territoriales furent présentées à la fois par des délégations arabes et juives et d'autre part, parce que l'ancien Empire ottoman devait être réparti entre les puissances victorieuses. Par conséquent, la question ne fut pas réglée dans les délais de la conférence de Paris.

Ce qui arriva à la conférence de Paris et qui façonna la progression des événements que nous considérons ici fut la création de la Société des Nations qui, dans l'article 22 de son Pacte, prévit la mise en place d'un système de mandat servant de fiducie pour les vieux territoires ottomans.

La prochaine grande étape sur la route de l'internationalisation du statut juridique et de la création d'une patrie juive fut la Conférence de San Remo, qui se tint à la Villa Devachan, à San Remo, en Italie, du 18 au 26 avril 1920. Elle fut une « prolongation » de la Conférence de paix de Paris de 1919 aux fins de traiter certaines de ces questions restées en suspens. L'objectif des quatre (sur cinq) membres du Conseil suprême des principales puissances alliées et associées réunis à San Remo (les Etats-Unis étant uniquement présents en tant qu'observateur, en raison de la nouvelle politique de non-intervention du président Woodrow Wilson) fut d'examiner les soumissions antérieures des demandeurs, de délibérer et de prendre des décisions sur la reconnaissance juridique de chaque revendication. En s'appuyant sur l'article 22 du Pacte de la Société des Nations, trois mandats furent créés, un pour la Syrie et le Liban (réparti en deux mandats ultérieurement), un pour la Mésopotamie (Irak) et un pour la Palestine. Le mandat pour la Palestine fut confié à la Grande Bretagne en tant que « mission sacrée de la civilisation » en matière d'« établissement en Palestine d'un foyer national pour le peuple juif ». Ce fut une résolution contraignante dotée de la force du droit international.

Dans deux des trois mandats originels, il fut reconnu que les peuples autochtones avaient la capacité de se gouverner et que la puissance mandataire n'assisterait qu'à la mise en place d'institutions gouvernementales, le cas échéant. Ce ne fut pas le cas pour la Palestine car, dans le cadre du mandat, elle était appelée à devenir la patrie (« foyer national ») du peuple juif. Bien que le peuple juif faisait partie de la population autochtone de la Palestine, la grande majorité de ceux-ci ne vivaient pas à l'époque encore dans le pays. Le mandat pour la Palestine était donc tout à fait différent des autres et énonça la manière dont le pays devait être régi par les Juifs en vue de la formation d'une nation viable au sein du territoire alors connu sous le nom de « Palestine ». Les obligations uniques du mandataire envers le peuple juif, dans le cadre de l'établissement de leur foyer national en Palestine donna ainsi un caractère sui generis (exceptionnel, unique en son genre) au mandat pour la Palestine.

Les limites de la « Palestine » visées dans les soumissions des demandeurs comprenaient des territoires à l'ouest et à l'est de la rivière du Jourdain. Les soumissions des demandeurs juifs précisèrent que le but ultime du mandat serait la « création d'une communauté autonome », étant clairement entendu « que rien ne sera fait qui puisse causer préjudice aux droits civils et religieux des communautés non juives en Palestine ». Le mandat pour la Palestine qui en résulta, approuvé par le Conseil de la Société des Nations en juillet 1922, fut un traité international et, à ce titre, fut juridiquement contraignant.

La décision prise à San Remo fut un grand tournant dans l'histoire du peuple juif qui avait été un peuple apatride depuis environ deux mille ans. Selon les propres mots de Chaïm Weizmann, président de l'Organisation sioniste nouvellement formée, et premier président en devenir de l'Etat d'Israël : « la reconnaissance de nos droits en Palestine est énoncée dans le traité avec la Turquie, et fait partie intégrante du droit international. Cela est l'événement politique le plus mémorable dans toute l'histoire de notre mouvement, et il n'est peut-être pas exagéré de dire, dans toute l'histoire de notre peuple depuis l'exil. » En outre, la résolution de San Remo « couronne la déclaration Balfour britannique en l'adoptant dans le cadre de la loi des nations du monde ».

La politique visant à donner effet au mandat pour la Palestine fut cohérente avec la Déclaration Balfour, car elle reconnaissait substantiellement d'une part les liens historiques, culturels et religieux du peuple juif avec la Terre Sainte, et même plus forte que la Déclaration en introduisant le principe fondamental que la Palestine devait être reconstituée comme le foyer national du peuple juif. Il est particulièrement pertinent de souligner l'incorporation dans les termes du mandat (à travers l'article 2) du principe fondamental énoncé dans le préambule de cet accord international que : « la reconnaissance a ainsi été accordée à la relation historique du peuple juif avec la Palestine et aux motifs de reconstitution de leur foyer national dans ce pays ».

L'objectif principal du mandat était de mettre en place un foyer national pour le peuple juif, sur leur terre ancestrale, y compris pour le peuple juif dispersé dans le monde entier. Le peuple arabe, exerçant déjà une souveraineté dans un certain nombre d'Etats, reçut la garantie de la protection de leurs droits civils et religieux sous le mandat aussi longtemps qu'ils souhaitaient rester, même après la création finale de l'Etat d'Israël en 1948. Par ailleurs, la Transjordanie fut entretemps ajoutée en tant que territoire sous souveraineté arabe et soustraite du territoire sous mandat en question par les britanniques, avant la signature effective du mandat en 1922 (voir ci-dessous).

Lorsque le conseil de la Société des Nations approuva le mandat pour la Palestine en juillet 1922, il devint contraignant pour l'ensemble des 51 membres de la Société. Cet acte de la Société permit d'une part la réalisation ultime du rêve caressé depuis longtemps de la restauration du peuple juif sur leur terre ancestrale et d'autre part valida l'existence de faits et événements historiques reliant le peuple juif à la Palestine. Pour les membres du Conseil suprême, lesdits faits historiques étaient considérés comme acceptés et instaurés. Selon les termes de Neville Barbour : « En 1922, la sanction internationale a été accordée à la Déclaration Balfour par la publication du mandat pour la Palestine ».

Les droits accordés au peuple juif dans le mandat pour la Palestine entrèrent en vigueur dans toute la Palestine. Il s'ensuivit donc que les droits légaux de la souveraineté des demandeurs sur la vieille ville de Jérusalem découlèrent aussi des décisions du Conseil suprême des principales puissances alliées à San Remo et des termes du mandat pour la Palestine approuvés par le Conseil de la Société des Nations.

En Mars 1921, au Caire, la Grande-Bretagne décida de répartir le territoire sous mandat de la Palestine pour des raisons politiques internationales qui lui étaient propres. L'article 25 du mandat accordait à la Puissance mandataire le pouvoir de différer ou de refuser la plupart

des termes du mandat pour les terrains se situant à l'est du Jourdain
(« Transjordanie »). La Grande-Bretagne, en tant que Puissance mandataire, exerça ce droit.

Pour l'ancien ambassadeur de l'ONU, le professeur Yehuda Blum
Zvi, les droits acquis par le peuple arabe de Palestine par rapport au
principe d'auto-détermination furent respectés du fait de ce premier
partage de la Palestine, approuvé par le Conseil de la Société des
Nations en 1922. Selon le professeur Blum : « Les Arabes palestiniens
ont bénéficié, depuis longtemps déjà, de l'auto-détermination dans
leur propre État : l'État arabe palestinien de Jordanie ». (Il convient
ici de souligner que dans une lettre apparemment écrite le 17 Janvier
1921 adressée au secrétaire privé de Churchill, Col. T.E. Lawrence
(« Lawrence d'Arabie ») a rapporté qu'en échange de la souveraineté
arabe en Irak, Transjordanie et Syrie, le fils aîné du Roi Hussein, Emir
Feisal, un homme connu, d'après Lawrence, pour garder sa parole,
avait « accepté de renoncer à toutes les prétentions de son père pour la
Palestine ».)

Après ce partage, Churchill, secrétaire colonial britannique de
l'époque, réaffirma immédiatement l'engagement de la Grande-
Bretagne à donner effet à la politique de la Déclaration Balfour dans
toutes les autres parties du territoire couvertes par le mandat pour la
Palestine à l'ouest du Jourdain. Cet engagement comprenait la région
de Jérusalem et de sa vieille ville. Selon les propres mots de Churchill
: « Il est manifeste et équitable que les Juifs qui sont dispersés par-
tout dans le monde devraient avoir un centre national et un foyer
national, que certains d'entre eux pourraient rejoindre. Et où d'autre
cela pourrait-il être que la terre de Palestine avec laquelle ils ont des
liens intimes et profonds depuis plus de 3000 ans ? »

Ainsi, en résumé, les fondements principaux en droit international
de la revendication «juridique» fondée sur des « droits historiques »
ou « titre historique » du peuple juif à l'égard de la Palestine sont les
décisions de San Remo en avril 1920, et le mandat pour la Palestine en
juillet 1922. Ceux-ci furent approuvés par le Conseil de la Société des
Nations et la signature fut apposée par les mêmes principales puissances alliées, ceci en faisant néanmoins un traité international contraignant pour tous les Etats membres. Les fondements se reflétèrent
également dans le Pacte de la Société des Nations lui-même (Art. 22).

Partie II : La question d'une déclaration unilatérale d'un Etat de Palestine

De nombreuses années séparent l'adoption du mandat en 1922 et la création de l'Etat d'Israël en 1948. Un évènement qui précipita la création de l'Etat hébreu fut le vote par l'Assemblée générale de l'ONU en 1947 du partage de la Palestine (Résolution 181 (II)), recommandant l'établissement d'un Etat juif ainsi que d'un Etat arabe au sein de ce territoire. Bien que les résolutions de l'Assemblée générale de l'ONU ne sont pas plus que des recommandations, sans aucune force contraignante sur le plan juridique, les Juifs acceptèrent le plan de partage, alors que les Arabes le rejetèrent. Le Royaume-Uni renonça à son rôle de Puissance mandataire et se retira du territoire le 14 Mai 1948. A cette date, prenant effet à minuit, les Juifs décrétèrent l'Etat d'Israël.

Le lendemain, les armées des cinq nations arabes voisines attaquèrent le nouvel Etat juif (la guerre d'indépendance d'Israël). Les Arabes rencontrèrent une défaite inopinée, alors que la Jordanie annexait illégalement la Judée et la Samarie. En 1967, Israël regagna le contrôle de son territoire mandaté dans une guerre de légitime défense, la guerre des Six Jours.

Malgré ces événements qui sont survenus depuis et qui ont remis en cause sa pertinence, notamment, la réalisation de son objet principal, la création d'un Etat juif, certains aspects fondamentaux du mandat restent valides et juridiquement contraignants et sont hautement pertinents dans la détermination des « questions essentielles » devant être négociées entre les deux parties concernant le « statut permanent » (ou « statut définitif ») de Jérusalem et de la « Cisjordanie ».

Pour remettre la situation en perspective, en ce qui concerne les structures légales internationales entourant la question de la déclaration unilatérale d'un Etat palestinien ayant pour capitale la partie orientale de Jérusalem, il est peut-être nécessaire d'aller au-delà de la loi, *per se*, afin de considérer l'impact de l'opinion publique sur la formulation du droit international tant coutumier que codifié. De la même façon, il faut attirer l'attention sur le degré auquel la résolution équitable des « questions essentielles » du conflit actuel, opposant les Israéliens et les Arabes palestiniens, peut être exacerbée à cause d'une hyperbole linguistique, d'une distorsion des faits ou d'une manoeuvre purement politique et d'une rhétorique calculée. Une certaine partie de cette rhétorique nécessite d'être analysée à la lumière de la terminologie légale et de la précision juridique. Sinon, cela peut facilement conduire à de grossières distorsions de la vérité et, en conséquence à des réponses juridiques malavisées. Prenons comme exemple, l'identité « palestinienne ». Lors de la décision de San Remo et du mandat pour la Palestine qui en a résulté, le territoire alors connu sous le nom de la « Palestine » était désigné uniquement et expressément dans le but de « reconstituer » le « foyer national » du peuple juif. Bien qu'un soin particulier ait été porté pour que les droits des Arabes et des autres habitants soient protégés, seul le peuple Juif se trouvait sans « patrie ». En effet, ceci était l'objet même du mandat pour la Palestine et de son prédécesseur, la Déclaration Balfour. A l'époque du mandat, il aurait été plus juste de se référer aux « Juifs palestiniens » et aux « Arabes palestiniens » (de même que pour de nombreux autres habitants non-juifs). Mais suite à la création de l'Etat d'Israël, les Juifs palestiniens conservèrent leur ancien nom d'« Israéliens » alors que les non-juifs (la plupart étant arabes) s'approprièrent le nom de « Palestiniens ». Ceci a eu comme résultat que ces derniers sont souvent considérés à tort comme les habitants de droit du pays. En réalité, le pays nommé « Palestine » recouvre le territoire que le peuple juif avait nommé la « Terre sainte » bien avant que le nom « Palestine » n'ait été utilisé pour la première fois par les Grecs et les Romains. En vérité, le territoire connu autrefois sous le nom de la « Palestine » n'a jamais, que ce soit depuis ou avant la première référence à ce nom, été ou désigné une nation arabe. Mais cette nomenclature s'accompagne d'un important impact psychologique en sous-entendant que les premiers habitants arabes de la Palestine sont les vrais « Palestiniens » et qu'ils sont les seuls à appartenir à la « Palestine ».

En ce qui concerne la question relative aux réfugiés, la définition légale de « réfugié » est « une personne qui fuit ou qui est expulsée d'un pays, principalement en raison d'une persécution et qui cherche refuge dans un autre pays » (définition traduite de l'anglais, tirée du dictionnaire du droit juridique de Black). La situation actuelle de tous ceux qui vivent dans des camps de réfugiés est réellement dramatique et suscite de droit la compassion du monde entier. Mais la plupart des Palestiniens identifiés comme « réfugiés » ont plus d'une génération d'écart avec les évènements qui ont contraint les générations précédentes à fuir. Le statut d'Etat a été accordé à de vastes territoires arabes il y a plusieurs générations et ces derniers pourraient aisément accueillir tous ces « réfugiés » infortunés, qui sont exhibés depuis six décennies au lieu d'être intégrés en tant que membres productifs de la société au sein de leur propre peuple. En plus des autres territoires mandatés à San Remo ayant acquis le statut d'Etat avant Israël, et qui auraient très bien pu intégrer leurs frères arabes, la Transjordanie avait quant à elle été divisée spécialement pour les Arabes palestiniens qui étaient sur le territoire désigné à l'origine comme étant le foyer national du peuple Juif. Un « nouvel Etat » avait ainsi déjà été attribué aux Arabes au sein de la « Palestine ». Le droit international n'a jamais eu à débattre de la question relative à l'« héritage » du statut de réfugié, une telle situation étant unique dans l'histoire humaine.

Quant à l'usage terminologique des « lignes de 1967 » comme point de référence d'un éventuel nouvel Etat Palestinien, il est constamment fait mention du retour aux « frontières de 1967 ». Tout d'abord, cette terminologie est juridiquement incorrecte. Le mot « frontières » se réfère en droit international à « frontières nationales », ce que les « lignes » de 1967 ne sont décidément pas. La définition d'une « frontière » en droit international est « une limite entre une nation (ou une subdivision politique de celle-ci) et une autre » (définition traduite de l'anglais, tirée du dictionnaire de droit américain de Black). De telles frontières nationales n'ont jamais été établies lors de la création de l'Etat d'Israël. Les « lignes » de 1967 sont simplement des lignes militaires à ne pas franchir (« lignes de démarcation de l'armistice ») qui datent de la Guerre d'Indépendance d'Israël de 1948. Ces « lignes » ont été expressément répétées dans de nombreux accords d'armistice israélo-palestiniens afin de ne pas être confondues avec les frontières nationales ou d'éviter de porter préjudice aux futures négociations bilatérales s'y rapportant. Les lignes d'armistice de 1949 sont restées valides jusqu'à l'éclatement de la guerre des Six Jours de 1967. Les associer à la guerre de 1967, durant laquelle le territoire perdu fut récupéré par les forces de défense d'Israël qui avaient été prises d'assaut, en les nommant « frontières de 1967 » au lieu de lignes d'armistice de 1949, a amplifié la notion erronée que ces « frontières » avaient été acquises illégalement, nuisant ainsi aux aboutissements des négociations. Eugene Rostow, le secrétaire d'Etat adjoint américain chargé des affaires politiques en 1967 et un des rédacteurs de la résolution 242 du Conseil de sécurité des Nations-Unies de 1967 dans le domaine de « la sécurité » des frontières, a indiqué en 1990, que cette résolution ainsi que la Résolution 338 du Conseil de sécurité : « …reposaient sur deux principes : Israël est autorisé à administrer le territoire jusqu'à ce que ces voisins arabes fassent la paix ; et lorsque celle-ci sera acquise, Israël devra se retirer dans les limites « des frontières sécurisées et reconnues », qui ne doivent pas nécessairement être les mêmes que les lignes de démarcation de l'armistice de 1949 ». En résumé, les lignes de 1967 ne sont pas du tout des « frontières », et ce mot ne devrait pas être utilisé pour créer ou perpétuer l'impression qu'Israël a transgressé les frontières d'un autre état de manière illégale, alors qu'il est évident que cela n'est pas le cas.

De même, si l'on considère les territoires contestés, l'usage répandu des mots « territoires occupés » plutôt que « territoires contestés » (ce qu'ils sont à proprement parler) s'accompagne d'un impact psychologique majeur qui peut avoir de véritables répercussions de toutes sortes y compris juridiques. De plus, cette terminologie et ce qu'elle tend à insinuer (« occupation belligérante ») ignore totalement le sens de la terminologie utilisé dans le traité international et de fait, ignore le sens donné au mot « reconstitué », tel qu'il figurait dans le mandat pour la Palestine. Territoire reconstitué exclut la notion d'«occupation belligérante», même si les frontières nationales permanentes n'ont pas encore été négociées. Un état ne peut pas, par définition, être « une puissance occupante belligérante » dans un territoire qui est en train d'être « reconstitué » en son nom, conformément aux dispositions d'un instrument juridiquement contraignant de droit international. « Une occupation se produit lorsqu'un état belligérant envahit le territoire d'un autre état avec l'intention d'occuper le territoire ne serait-ce que temporairement » (définition traduite de l'anglais, tirée de l'encyclopédie de droit américain de West.) Le territoire qu'Israël a récupéré en 1967 n'a jamais été de droit « le territoire d'un autre état », et Israël ne l'a en aucun cas obtenu en menant une guerre d'agression. En réalité, ce territoire avait été spécifiquement désigné en tant que foyer national du peuple juif, conformément au mandat juridiquement contraignant pour la Palestine de 1922.

Un corollaire direct est la question des colonies. Les sensibilités qui règnent autour de ce problème sont exacerbées par le fait même que la légalité ou l'illégalité de ces colonies est basée sur des facteurs qui ne suivent pas les normes du droit international prescrites mais aussi en raison de la nature unique et complexe du cas israélien. Par exemple, alors qu'il est souvent proclamé que telle colonie viole l'article 49 de la Convention de Genève (IV), il faut préciser que l'incorporation de cet article dans la convention avait un objectif autre que celui de régir les circonstances aujourd'hui présentes en Israël. L'intention des rédacteurs était de protéger les civils vulnérables en temps de conflit armé en créant un instrument juridique international qui déclarerait illicite toute déportation forcée telle que celle qui fut subie par plus de 40 million d'allemands, de soviétiques, de polonais, d'ukrainiens, de hongrois et autres, immédiatement après la deuxième guerre mondiale. Dans le cas d'Israël, conformément au droit international tel qu'il figurait dans le mandat pour la Palestine, les Juifs était autorisés et même encouragés à s'installer dans toutes les régions de la Palestine, mais n'étaient pas déportés ou transférés de force. Par conséquent, déclarer que les colonies israéliennes de Judée, de Samarie et de « Jérusalem-Est » sont « illégales » n'est pas une application pertinente de la quatrième Convention de Genève.

La question de Jérusalem est peut-être la plus instable de toutes. Etant donné le caractère sacré que possède la ville pour beaucoup de personnes, il est devenu évident que les positions adoptées par Israël et les Palestiniens concernant la vieille ville sont pratiquement irréconciliables. Cela est attesté par le fait qu'elles ne furent pas mentionnées dans l'accord-cadre pour la paix au Moyen-Orient, signé par Israël et l'Égypte, lors des accords de Camp David en 1978. Dans ce dernier cas, la ville de Jérusalem était à l'ordre du jour, mais fut laissée de côté dans les accords définitifs, les deux parties étant incapables de résoudre leurs différences fondamentales sur ce problème particulièrement compliqué. L'échec du sommet de Camp David en juillet 2000 souligna à nouveau l'importance de la question de Jérusalem et de sa vieille ville.

Pour en venir au rôle des Nations Unies dans le débat actuel, on ne doit pas oublier que conformément à la Charte des Nations Unies, l'Assemblée générale des Nations Unies n'a pas le pouvoir de mettre en place des mesures juridiques contraignantes. Les résolutions de l'Assemblée générale ont seulement le pouvoir de recommander et n'ont pas force de loi. Ainsi, s'il devait y avoir une résolution qui « reconnait » les « Arabes palestiniens » en tant qu'entité politique et/ ou étatique, cela ne constituerait pas en soi un Etat palestinien conformément au droit international, pas plus que la résolution 181 (II) de 1947 (plan de partage de la Palestine) n'a créé l'Etat d'Israël.

De plus, des engagements ont été pris des deux côtés afin de mener des négociations relatives à propos du « statut permanent » Les dirigeants de l'OLP (Organisation de libération de la Palestine) s'engagèrent en 1993 à soumettre pour ainsi dire toutes les questions importantes relatives au « statut permanent » uniquement par la voie de la négociation. En vertu de l'accord intérimaire de 1995 (Oslo II), les parties s'engagèrent à ne pas agir unilatéralement pour modifier le statut des territoires avant de connaître les aboutissements des négociations concernant le statut permanent. Il était clairement stipulé et convenu que : « ... aucune partie ne doit initier ou prendre des mesures qui auront pour effet de modifier le statut de la Cisjordanie et de la bande de Gaza tant que les négociations concernant le statut permanent n'ont pas encore abouti ».

Un Etat palestinien déclaré de façon unilatérale serait alors en opposition avec les engagements figurant dans l'instrument juridique international ainsi que dans des documents publiés officiellement et des déclarations publiques.

En somme, ce conflit n'est pas un conflit traditionnel portant sur les frontières car celles-ci, en réalité, ne sont pas le véritable problème, comme en témoigne le fait même que les frontières nationales sont restées indéterminées pendant si longtemps. Il s'agit d'un conflit qui concerne les droits historiques et le besoin reconnu internationalement pour un "peuple" unifié d'avoir un endroit (et un espace territorial) où il pourrait revenir « à la maison » après quelques deux mille ans « d'apatridie » et de séparation avec le pays de ses ancêtres : le seul endroit qu'il qualifie de « saint » et la seule Terre qu'il n'a jamais cessé d'appeler sa « patrie ».

KURZFASSUNG
ÜBERSETZUNG: Maßgebend ist ausschließlich die ursprüngliche englische Fassung

Teil I: Grundlagen der völkerrechtlich verankerten Rechte der Juden und des Staates Israel

Das Völkerrecht behandelt, wie jedes Recht, immer zwei Seiten einer Frage. Andernfalls wären gesetzliche Lösungen kaum erforderlich. Zudem glauben in jedem Konflikt beide Seiten, das Recht auf ihrer Seite zu haben. Zumindest denken sie, sie hätten die nötigen Mittel, um dies zu beweisen. Folglich entsteht Recht nie in einem Vakuum, sondern vielmehr, wenn sich hierfür eine ausreichend gravierende Notwendigkeit zeigt.

Durch die Ereignisse des Ersten Weltkrieges erkannte man 1917 eine
solche Notwendigkeit. Und es erhob sich eine Stimme. Es ging um die
Notwendigkeit, den seit ca. 2000 Jahren auf der Erde verstreut lebenden Juden eine nationale Heimstätte zu geben. Die Stimme war die von
Lord Balfour, der sich im Namen des britischen Kriegskabinetts für die
Juden weltweit einsetzte. Diese dringliche Notwendigkeit fand ihren
offiziellen Ausdruck in der Balfour-Erklärung von 1917.
Die *Balfour-Erklärung* war eine *politische* Aussage ohne rechtliche
Bindung. Außerdem war sie nicht *international*. Dennoch stellte sie
in der Geschichte des verstreut lebenden jüdischen Volkes einen
wichtigen Wendepunkt dar: Sie gab ihm eine Hoffnung, letztlich
seine stets am Leben gebliebene Sehnsucht nach seinem angestammten Heiligen Land zu erfüllen. Die Erklärung stärkte international
das Bewusstsein dafür, dass ein staatenloses Volk einer "nationalen Heimat" bedarf, in die es zurückkehren konnte. Von enormer
Bedeutung war die offizielle Anerkennung der überaus wichtigen
historischen, religiösen und *kulturellen* Verbindungen der Juden
zum Land ihrer Vorväter, zu dem Land, das seit den Griechen und
Römern als "Palästina" bekannt ist.

Die Sache war gerecht und das Konzept begründet. Darum galt es,
eine Möglichkeit zu suchen, den Inhalt dieser Erklärung auf die Ebene
des Völkerrechts zu heben. Folglich widmete sich der Oberste Rat der
Alliierten und Assoziierten Großmächte (Großbritannien, Frankreich,
Italien, Japan und die Vereinigten Staaten) der Angelegenheit auf
der Pariser Friedenskonferenz von 1919. Das Problem gestaltete sich
indes in dem Maße immer komplexer, in dem sowohl arabische, als
auch jüdische Delegationen territoriale Ansprüche geltend machten,
während das alte Osmanische Reich unter den Siegermächten aufgeteilt wurde. Deshalb ließ sich die Frage auch nicht innerhalb des
Zeitrahmens der Pariser Konferenz lösen.

Auf der Pariser Konferenz entstand jedoch der *Völkerbund*, was den
Lauf der hier betrachteten Ereignisse mit beeinflusste. Artikel 22 der
Satzung des Völkerbundes sah nämlich vor, für die alten osmanischen
Gebiete ein Mandatsystem mit Treuhandfunktion zu schaffen.
Der nächste wichtige Meilenstein zum völkerrechtlichen
Status und zu einer nationalen Heimstätte für die Juden war die
Konferenz von San Remo vom 18. bis zum 26. April 1920 in der Villa
Devachan im italienischen San Remo. Sie galt als eine "Fortsetzung"
der Pariser Friedenskonferenz von 1919 und sollte einige dieser

außergewöhnlichen Themen in Angriff nehmen. In San Remo
kamen vier (der fünf) Mitglieder des Obersten Rates der Alliierten
und Assoziierten Großmächte zusammen (die Vereinigten Staaten
waren aufgrund der neuen Politik der Nichteinmischung ihres
Präsidenten Woodrow Wilson nur als Beobachter anwesen). Sie
wollten die Eingaben der Anspruchsteller begutachten, beratschlagen
und Entscheidungen über die rechtliche Anerkennung einer jeden
einzelnen Forderung treffen. Das Ergebnis stützte sich auf Artikel 22
der Satzung des Völkerbundes : die Einrichtung dreier Mandate, eines
über Syrien und den Libanon (das später in zwei Mandate aufgeteilt
wurde), eines über Mesopotamien (Irak) sowie eines über Palästina.
Das *Mandat für Palästina* wurde Grossbritannin anvertraut als "hei-
lige Aufgabe der Zivilisation" mit dem Ziel der "Schaffung einer nationalen Heimstätte für die Juden in Palästina". Es handelte sich um
eine bindende Resolution mit der gesamten Kraft des Völkerrechts.

Zwei der drei Mandate gingen davon aus, dass die einheimische
Bevölkerung imstande wäre, sich selbst zu regieren. Die Mandatsmacht
würde bei Bedarf lediglich helfen, die Regierungsinstitutionen zu
gründen. Das galt hingegen nicht für Palästina: Palästina sollte dem
Mandat nach die Heimat ("nationale Heimstätte") der Juden werden.
Obwohl Juden der einheimischen Bevölkerung Palästinas angehörten,
lebten die allermeisten von ihnen zu diesem Zeitpunkt noch nicht im
Lande. Das Mandat für Palästina unterschied sich daher recht deutlich
von den anderen. Es legte fest, wie das Land von Juden zu besiedeln wäre,
um innerhalb des als "Palästina" bekannten Gebietes eine lebensfähige
Nation zu bilden. Die *einmaligen* Verpflichtungen des Mandatsträgers
gegenüber dem jüdischen Volk hinsichtlich der Schaffung ihrer nationalen Heimstätte in Palästina verliehen dem Mandat für Palästina somit
einen *Charakter sui generis* (in seiner Art einzigartig).

Die Grenzen des "Palästinas", auf das sich die Anspruchsteller in
ihren Anträgen bezogen, umfasste Gebiete *westlich und östlich* des
Jordans. Die Eingaben der jüdischen Antragsteller spezifizierten,
dass der Endzweck des Mandates darin bestünde, "ein autonomes
Gemeinwesen" zu schaffen, vorausgesetzt, "dass nichts unternommen
werden dürfe, das die bürgerlichen und religiösen Rechte der sich
gegenwärtig in Palästina befindlichen nicht-jüdischen Gemeinschaften
beeinträchtigen könnte". Hieraus ergab sich das Mandat für Palästina.
Der Rat des Völkerbundes billigte es im Juli 1922. Das Mandat war ein
völkerrechtlicher Vertrag und als solcher rechtlich bindend.

Die in San Remo getroffene Entscheidung war ein Wendepunkt in

Abstract 91

der Geschichte des jüdischen Volkes, das rund zweitausend Jahre lang
keine Heimat hatte.

Chaim Weizmann, Präsident der neu gegründeten
Zionistischen Organisation und später erster Präsident des Staates Israel,
drückte es so aus: "Diese Anerkennung unserer Rechte ist im Vertrag mit
der Türkei verkörpert und Teil des Völkerrechts geworden. Dies ist das
folgenreichste politische Ereignis in der gesamten Geschichte unserer
Bewegung. Vielleicht kann man ohne Übertreibung sagen, es ist das
folgenreichste politische Ereignis in der gesamten Geschichte unseres
Volkes seit seiner Verbannung." Darüber hinaus ist die Resolution von
San Remo "die Krönung der britischen [Balfour]-Erklärung, da sie sie
zum Bestandteil des Rechts der Nationen dieser Welt machte".

Die Politik, die mit dem Mandat für Palästina in Kraft treten sollte,
stimmte mit der Balfour-Erklärung überein: Sie anerkannte umfas-
send die *historischen, kulturellen und religiösen* Verbindungen des
jüdischen Volkes mit dem Heiligen Land, und dies noch viel stärker
als die [Balfour]-Erklärung durch die Einführung des grundleg-
enden Prinzips, demzufolge Palästina als nationale Heimstätte des
jüdischen Volkes *wiederherzustellen sei.* Es ist besonders relevant,
den Einbezug des fundamentalen Prinzips aus der Präambel dieses
völkerrechtlichen Vertrages in das Mandat (durch Artikel 2) zu
unterstreichen: "Die historische Verbindung des jüdischen Volkes mit
Palästina und mit dem Boden zur *Wiederherstellung* der nationalen
Heimstätte der Juden in diesem Land wurde so anerkannt".

*Hauptziel des Mandats war, eine nationale Heimstätte für das
jüdische Volk*—einschließlich der *weltweit* verstreut lebenden Juden—
in ihrer angestammten Heimat zu schaffen. Den arabischen Menschen,
die ihre Souveränität bereits in mehreren Staaten ausübten, garan-
tierte das Mandat ihre bürgerlichen und religiösen Rechte—solange
sie bleiben wollten und das selbst nach der endgültigen Gründung des
Staates Israel 1948. Darüber hinaus kam mittlerweile Transjordanien
als Gebiet unter arabischer Souveränität hinzu. Die Briten hatten
Transjordanien *direkt aus dem bewussten Mandatsgebiet heraus
geschaffen,* bevor das Mandat 1922 unterzeichnet worden war (siehe
unten).

Als der Rat des Völkerbundes das Mandat für Palästina im Juli
1922 billigte, wurde es für alle 51 Mitglieder des Bundes bindend.
Dieser Akt des Völkerbundes ermöglichte es, den lang gehegten
Traum der *Wiederherstellung* der jüdischen Nation *in ihrem angestammten Land* wahr zu machen. *Er bestätigte auch die beste-
henden historischen Tatsachen und Ereignisse, die das jüdische*

Volk mit Palästina verbinden. Die Mitglieder des Obersten Rates der Alliierten und der Rat des Völkebundes erachteten diese *historischen Tatsachen als akzeptiert und anerkannt.* Neville Barbour beschrieb es so: *"1922 wurde der Balfour-Erklärung durch die Verabschiedung des Palästinamandates internationale Anerkennung verliehen."* Die dem jüdischen Volk im Mandat für Palästina garantierten Rechte sollten in *ganz Palästina* gelten. Somit sind die *gesetzlichen Rechte* der Anspruchsteller auf Souveränität der *Altstadt von Jerusalem* gleichfalls aus den Beschlüssen des Obersten Rates der Großmächte in San Remo sowie aus den Bestimmungen des Mandates für Palästina, das der Rat des Völkerbundes billigte, ableitbar.

Im März 1921 beschloss Großbritannien in Kairo aus eigenen politischen Gründen, das Mandatsgebiet von Palästina aufzuteilen. Artikel 25 des Mandats gestattete es der Mandatsmacht, die meisten Bestimmungen des Mandats im Gebiet östlich des Jordans ("Transjordanien") auszusetzen oder nicht zu realisieren. Dieses Recht übte Großbritannien als Mandatsmacht damals aus.

Für den ehemaligen UNO-Botschafter, Professor Yehuda Zvi Blum, *wurden die den arabischen Einwohnern Palästinas hinsichtlich des Selbstbestimmungsprinzips verbrieften Rechte als Ergebnis dieser ersten, vom Rat des Völkerbundes 1922 gebilligten Teilung Palästinas erfüllt. Professor Blum führte dazu im Jahre 1980 aus: "Die palästinensischen Araber genießen seit langem ihre Selbstbestimmung in ihrem eigenen Staat: dem palästinensischen arabischen Staat Jordanien".* (Erwähnenswert ist, dass Colonel T.E. Lawrence ("von Arabien") in einem Brief (anscheinend vom 17. Januar 1921) an Churchills Privatsekretär berichtet hatte, dass König Husseins ältester Sohn, Emir Feisal – ein Mann, der nach Aussage von Lawrence dafür bekannt war, sein Wort zu halten – im Gegenzug für die arabische Souveränität im Irak, in Transjordanien und in Syrien *"zugestimmt [hat], alle Ansprüche seines Vaters auf Palästina aufzugeben".*)

Nach dieser Teilung bestätigte Churchill – damals britischer Kolonialsekretär – umgehend Großbritanniens Bestreben, die Richtlinien der Balfour-Erklärung in *allen anderen Teilen des Gebietes umzusetzen, die das* Mandat für Palästina westlich des Jordans abdeckte. *Dieses Versprechen beinhaltete das Gebiet Jerusalem und seine Altstadt.* Churchill erklärte selbst: "Es ist eindeutig richtig, dass die überall auf der Welt verstreut lebenden Juden ein nationales Zentrum und eine nationale Heimstätte benötigen, wo einige von ihnen wieder zusammenleben können. Woanders könnte dies geschehen als im Land Palästina, mit dem sie seit mehr als 3000 Jahren eng und fest verbunden sind?"

Die Hauptgrundlagen im Völkerrecht für den "rechtlichen" Anspruch des jüdischen Volkes auf Palästina - basierend auf "historischen Rechten" oder "historischem Anspruch"- bilden somit, kurz gesagt, die Beschlüsse von San Remo vom April 1920, das Mandat für Palästina vom Juli 1922, das der Rat des Völkerbundes billigte und das die Unterschriften eben dieser alliierten Großmächte trägt und es so zu einem für alle Mitgliedsstaaten bindenden völkerrechtlichen Vertrag macht, *sowie die Satzung des Völkerbundes selbst (Art. 22).*

TEIL II: DIE FRAGE EINER EINSEITIGEN ERKLÄRUNG EINES PALÄSTINENSISCHEN STAATES

Seit Annahme des Mandats 1922 vergingen vielen Jahre bis zur Gründung des Staates Israel im Jahre 1948. Ein Ereignis, das die Staatsgründung Israels beschleunigte, war 1947 die Zustimmung der UN-Generalversammlung zu einer Teilung Palästinas (Resolution 181 (II)), die empfahl, auf diesem Territorium einen jüdischen und einen arabischen Staat zu errichten. Obschon Resolutionen der UN-Generalversammlung rechtlich nur Empfehlungen darstellen und somit nicht rechtsverbindlich sind, nahmen die Juden den Teilungsplan an, wogegen die Araber ihn ablehnten. Grossbritannien beendete seine Rolle als Mandatsmacht und zog sich am 14. Mai 1948 aus dem Gebiet zurück. Gleichentags – mit Wirkung ab Mitternacht –riefen die Juden den Staat Israel aus.

Am folgenden Tag griffen die Armeen von fünf umliegenden arabischen Nationen den neugegründeten jüdischen Staat an (Israelischer Unabhängigkeitskrieg). Die Araber erlitten eine unerwartete Niederlage, obgleich Jordanien rechtswidrig Judäa und Samaria annektierte. Israel erlangte die Kontrolle über dieses ihm zugesprochene Gebiet in einem Verteidigungskrieg zurück, dem Sechstagekrieg von 1967.

Trotz dieser eingetretenen Ereignisse, die seither seine andauernde Relevanz beeinflusst haben - nicht zuletzt die Erfüllung seines Hauptzweckes, der Schaffung eines jüdischen Staates – bleiben bestimmte grundlegende Aspekte des Mandates gültig und rechtlich verbindlich. Sie sind überaus relevant, um jene "Kernfragen" zu bestimmen, die beide Parteien über den "dauerhaften Status" (oder den "endgültigen Status") von Jerusalem und der "Westbank" verhandeln müssen.

Wenn wir den völkerrechtlichen Rahmen um die Frage eines einseitig erklärten palästinensischen Staates mit Ost-Jerusalem als Hauptstadt betrachten, müssen wir für die richtige Perspektive vielleicht über das Recht *per se* hinausgehen. So können wir den Einfluss der öffentlichen Meinung auf die Auslegung des Völkergewohnheitsrechtes und des kodifizierten Völkerrechtes beurteilen. Entsprechend ist das Ausmaß zu beachten, in dem sprachliche Übertreibungen, verdrehte Tatsachen oder politische Manöver und kalkulierte Rhetorik gerechte Lösungen für die "Kernfragen" des heutigen Konfliktes zwischen Israel und dem arabischen Palästina behindern können. Ein Teil dieser Rhetorik ist unbedingt auf seine rechtlichen Begriffe und Genauigkeit zu analysieren. Andernfalls kann sie die Wahrheit rasch extrem verzerren, was wiederum unkluge völkerrechtliche Reaktionen bewirken könnte.

Nehmen wir beispielsweise die *"Palästinensische" Identität*. Beim Beschluss von San Remo und dem daraus resultierenden Mandat für Palästina war das damals als "Palästina" bekannte Gebiet ausdrücklich für die "Wiederherstellung" der "nationalen Heimstätte" einzig des jüdischen Volkes bestimmt. Man achtete darauf, die Rechte arabischer und anderer Einwohner zu schützen, doch waren nur die Juden ein Volk ohne "Heimat". Genau das war ja der eigentliche Zweck des Mandats für Palästina und dessen Vorgängerin, der Balfour-Erklärung. Zum Zeitpunkt des Mandats wäre es genauer gewesen, von "palästinensischen Juden" und "palästinensischen Arabern" (neben mehreren anderen nicht-jüdischen Einwohnern) zu sprechen. Da der Staat Israel entstand, beanspruchten die "palästinensischen Juden" jedoch wieder ihren uralten Namen "Israelis". Die Nichtjuden hingegen (vor allem Araber, aber nicht nur) nahmen den Namen "Palästinenser" an.

Als Folge davon werden sie nun oftmals irrtümlich für die rechtmäßigen Einwohner des Landes gehalten. In Wirklichkeit umfasst das Land "Palästina" ein Gebiet, das die Juden, lange bevor Griechen und Römer erstmals von "Palästina" sprachen, schon als "Heiliges Land" bezeichneten. Doch in Wahrheit war das einst als "Palästina" bekannte Gebiet niemals eine arabische Nation oder dazu bestimmt, eine solche zu sein – weder seitdem der Name "Palästina" verwendet wurde, noch davor. Doch die Bezeichnung "Palästina" hat eine große psychologische

Wirkung. Sie suggeriert: Die ehemaligen arabischen Bewohner seien die *wahren* "Palästinenser" und sie *allein gehörten* nach "Palästina".

Zur Flüchtlingsfrage: Per rechtlicher Definition ist ein "Flüchtling" eine Person, die—insbesondere durch Verfolgung—aus einem Land flieht oder vertrieben wurde und in einem anderen Land Schutz sucht" (Black's Law Dictionary). Die heutige Misere aller Menschen in Flüchtlingslagern ist wirklich bedauernswert. Sie weckt zu Recht das Mitleid der Welt. Doch für die meisten als "Flüchtlinge" betitelten Palästinenser gilt: Die Ereignisse, die zur Flucht einer Vorgeneration führten, liegen weit mehr als eine Generation zurück. Zudem erhielten große arabische Gebiete schon vor vielen Generationen ihre Eigenstaatlichkeit. Sie könnten ganz leicht all diese überaus unglücklichen "Flüchtlinge" aufnehmen, mit denen seit sechs Jahrzehnten ein Schauspiel veranstaltet wird, anstatt sie als produktive Mitglieder der Gesellschaft in ihr eigenes Volk zu integrieren. Die anderen San-Remo-Mandatsgebiete, die ihre Staatlichkeit vor Israel erhielten, hätten ihre arabischen Brüder problemlos aufnehmen können. *Darüber hinaus* wurde ja Transjordanien *ausdrücklich* für die palästinensischen Araber abgeteilt - aus jenem Gebiet also, das ursprünglich gänzlich als nationale Heimstätte für die Juden bestimmt war. *So entstand innerhalb des Gebietes "Palästinas" bereits ein legitimer "neuer Staat".* Nirgendwo sonst musste sich das Völkerrecht mit der Frage eines "ererbten" Flüchtlingsstatus auseinandersetzen. Diese Situation ist einzig in der Menschheitsgeschichte.

Zu den *"Linien von 1967"* als Bezugspunkt für einen möglichen neuen palästinensischen Staat: Hierbei spricht man ständig von einem Rückzug auf die *"Grenzen von 1967"*. Zunächst einmal ist dieser Begriff rechtlich inkorrekt. Das Völkerrecht versteht unter "Grenzen" im Allgemeinen "nationale Grenzen", und das sind die sog. "Linien" von 1967 eindeutig nicht. Die Definition einer "Grenze" nach dem Völkerrecht ist eine "Grenze zwischen einer Nation (oder einer politischen Untereinheit [besagter Nation]) und einer anderen Nation" (Black's Law Dictionary). Solche nationalen Grenzen wurden im vorliegenden Fall für den wiedergeborenen Staat Israel nie festgelegt. Die "Linien" von 1967 sind lediglich nicht zu überschreitende *militärische* Linien (Grenzlinien des Waffenstillstandes) aus Israels Unabhängigkeitskrieg von 1948. Von diesen "Linien" heißt es in *zahlreichen* israelisch-palästinensischen Waffenstillstandsvereinbarungen von 1949 *ausdrücklich*: Sie sind weder nationale Grenzen, noch dürfen sie zukünftige bilaterale Verhandlungen präjudizieren. Diese "Waffenstillstandslinien von 1949" galten bis zum Sechstagekrieg von 1967. Verknüpft man sie mit diesem Krieg – einem Krieg, in dem die angegriffenen israelischen Verteidigungsstreitkräfte verlorenes Territorium zurückeroberten – indem man sie "Grenzen von 1967" statt Waffenstillstandslinien von 1949 nennt, fördert man die irrige Auffassung von unrechtmäßigen "Grenzen". So präjudiziert man Problem und Ergebnis.

Eugene Rostow, 1967 Staatssekretär für politische Angelegenheiten und Mitverfasser der Resolution 242 des UNO-Sicherheitsrates über "sichere und geschützte" Grenzen, erklärte 1990, dass die besagte Resolution sowie die nachfolgende Resolution 338 des Sicherheitsrates "…auf zwei Prinzipien fußten: Israel darf das Gebiet solange verwalten, bis seine arabischen Nachbarn Frieden geschlossen haben, und wenn dies der Fall ist, muss sich Israel auf "sichere und anerkannte Grenzen" zurückziehen, die den Demarkationslinien des Waffenstillstands von 1949 nicht entsprechen müssen". Kurzum: Die Linien von 1967 sind *überhaupt keine* "Grenzen". Dieser Begriff sollte nicht verwendet werden, um den Eindruck zu erwecken und zu verewigen, Israel hätte die Grenzen eines anderen Staates illegal überschritten, was eindeutig nicht der Fall ist.

Genauso hat hinsichtlich der *umstrittenen Gebiete* die verbreitete Bezeichnung "besetztes Gebiet" statt "umstrittenes Gebiet" (was es tatsächlich auch ist) einen großen psychologischen Einfluss - mit potentiellen realen und sogar juristischen Komplikationen. Außerdem ignoriert diese Terminologie - und was sie tendenziell suggeriert ("kriegerische Okkupation") - völlig die Aussage des völkerrechtlichen Vertrags über eine *"Wiederherstellung"*, wie sie das Mandat für Palästina vorsieht. Ein *wiederhergestelltes* Gebiet schließt "eine kriegerische Okkupation" aus. Das gilt selbst dann, wenn dauerhafte nationale Grenzen noch auszuhandeln sind. Ein Staat kann per Definition keine "kriegerische Besatzungsmacht" in einem Gebiet sein, das in seinem Namen "wiederhergestellt" wird, folgt man den Bestimmungen eines rechtlich verbindlichen völkerrechtlichen Instruments. "Eine Okkupation ist gegeben, wenn ein kriegerischer Staat das Territorium eines anderen Staates überfällt, um dieses Territorium, zumindest zeitweise, zu behalten" (West's Encyclopedia of American Law.) Das von Israel 1967 zurückeroberte Gebiet jedoch war von Rechts wegen nie "Territorium eines anderen Staates". Israel hat es auch nicht durch einen Angriffskrieg erlangt. Vielmehr war es spezifisch als nationale Heimstätte für die Juden bestimmt, wie es das rechtlich verbindliche Mandat für Palästina 1922 festlegte.

Als logische Folgerung daraus ergibt sich ist die Frage der *Siedlungen.* Die Befindlichkeiten bei diesem Problem werden durch die schiere Tatsache verschärft, dass die Rechtmäßigkeit/ Unrechtmäßigkeit derartiger Siedlungen auf Faktoren beruht, die unter Umständen keinen festgeschriebenen, völkerrechtlichen Normen folgen, sondern vielmehr durch die Einmaligkeit des Falles Israel verkompliziert werden. So wird oft behauptet, die Siedlungen verletzten Artikel 49 der Genfer Konvention (IV). Besagter Artikel floss jedoch in die Konvention zu einem völlig anderen Zweck ein, als um mit Umstände wie denen im heutigen Israel zu umzugehen. Die Verfasser wollten *während bewaffneter Konflikte hilflose Zivilisten schützen.* Dazu schufen sie ein völkerrechtliches Instrument, das alle erzwungenen Deportationen wie die von über 40 Mio. Deutschen, Sowjetbürgern, Polen, Ukrainern, Ungarn und anderen, kurz nach dem 2. Weltkrieg erlittenen als unrechtmäßig erklären würde. Im Falle Israels *gestattete, ja ermutigte* das Völkerrecht unter dem Mandat für Palästina die Juden dazu, sich in *allen* Teilen Palästinas niederzulassen. Sie wurden aber *nicht* deportiert oder zwangsweise umgesiedelt. Bezeichnet man folglich die israelischen Siedlungen in "Ostjerusalem", Judäa und Samarien als illegal, so ist dies keine taugliche Anwendung der Vierten Genfer Konvention.

Die *Jerusalem-Frage* ist wohl die explosivste von allen. Die Stadt hat für so viele einen heiligen Status. Deshalb sind, wie sich herausstellte, die Positionen Israels und der Palästinenser zur Altstadt praktisch unvereinbar. Die Jerusalem-Frage blieb deshalb im "Rahmen für Frieden im Nahen Osten", der 1978 im Camp-David-Abkommen zwischen Israel und Ägypten vereinbart wurde, ausgeklammert. Hierbei stand Jerusalem zwar auf der Tagesordnung, floss aber nicht in die eigentlichen Abkommen ein. Der Grund: Die beiden Parteien konnten ihre grundsätzlichen Differenzen in dieser überaus belasteten Frage nicht lösen. Der Misserfolg des Gipfels von Camp David im Juli 2000 unterstrich erneut die Bedeutung von Jerusalem bzw. seiner Altstadt.

Betrachten wir die *Rolle der Vereinten Nationen* in der aktuellen Debatte. Dabei sollte man bedenken, dass die UNO-Generalversammlung gemäss UNO-Charta nicht ermächtigt ist, rechtlich verbindliche Beschlüsse zu treffen. Resolutionen der Generalversammlung erlauben nur Empfehlungen, die rechtlich unverbindlich sind. Sollte also einmal eine Resolution die "arabischen Palästinenser" als politische/staatliche Einheit "anerkennen", wäre dies an und für sich nach dem Völkerrecht keine Gründung eines palästinensischen Staates—ebenso wenig wie die Resolution 181 (II) (der UN-Teilungsplan) von 1947 den Staat Israel schuf.

Darüber hinaus haben sich beide Seiten zu *Verhandlungen über den "dauerhaften Status"* verpflichtet. Die PLO-Führung verpflichtete sich 1993 dazu, in praktisch allen wichtigen Fragen zum "dauerhaften Status" auf Verhandlungslösungen zu setzen. Nach dem Interimsabkommen (Oslo II) von 1995 verpflichteten sich die Parteien, *keine einseitigen Schritte zu unternehmen,* die den Status der Gebiete vor Vorliegen der Verhandlungergebnisse (zum dauerhaften Status) ändern würden. Es wurde eindeutig festgelegt und vereinbart, dass: "... *keine Seite* Schritte einleitet oder unternimmt, die den Status der Westbank und des Gaza-Streifens verändern, solange die *permanenten Verhandlungen zum dauerhaften Status* zu keinen Ergebnissen geführt haben".

Ein einseitig erklärter palästinensischer Staat würde deshalb gegen die Verpflichtungen verstoßen, die in einem völkerrechtlichen Instrument sowie in öffentlich erklärten und publizierten offiziellen Stellungsnahmen und Dokumenten verkörpert sind.

Zusammenfassend lässt sich feststellen: Dies ist kein herkömmlicher *Grenz*konflikt. Um Grenzen geht es im Grunde gar nicht. Das zeigt die Tatsache, dass nationale Grenzen über einen so langen Zeitraum gar nicht festgelegt wurden. Der Konflikt betrifft vielmehr historische Rechte und die international anerkannte Notwendigkeit, einen Ort (und ein Gebiet) zu schaffen, an den ein wieder vereinigtes "Volk" nach einer ca. 2000 Jahre dauernden "Staatenlosigkeit" und Trennung vom Land seiner Väter zurückkehren kann – dem einzigen Ort, den dieses Volk als "heilig" bezeichnet, und dem einzigen Land, das es je "Heimat" genannt hat.

ABSTRACT

TRADUZIONE: Solo la versione originale inglese fa fede

Parte I: Fondamenta dei Diritti Legali
Internazionali del Popolo Ebraico

e dello Stato di Israele

Nel diritto internazionale, come in ogni tipo di diritto, esistono sempre due lati di una questione. Se così non fosse, non ci sarebbe bisogno di soluzioni legali. Inoltre, entrambe le parti in qualsiasi conflitto ritengono di avere ragione, o almeno di avere i mezzi per comprovarlo. Di conseguenza, non esistono leggi create a vuoto; le leggi vengono create a seguito di un bisogno sufficientemente sentito. Nel 1917, a seguito degli eventi della Prima Guerra Mondiale, fu identificato un bisogno profondo e fu lanciato un appello. Il bisogno era quello del popolo ebraico, che era stato disperso in tutto il mondo per circa duemila anni, e che sentiva la necessità di avere un focolare nazionale. La voce era quella di Lord Balfour, che parlava a nome del Gabinetto di Guerra britannico a difesa del popolo ebraico in tutto il mondo. Questo stringente bisogno trovò espressione ufficiale nella Dichiarazione Balfour del 1917.

La *Dichiarazione Balfour* fu una dichiarazione di natura *politica*, senza autorità legale; inoltre *non* aveva valore *internazionale*. Non di meno, si trattò di un importante punto di svolta nella storia del popolo ebraico in diaspora, dandogli una speranza futura di vedere adempiuto l'immortale desiderio di ottenere la sua antica Terra Santa. Questa dichiarazione ottenne lo scopo di evidenziare a livello internazionale il bisogno di un popolo che non aveva patria di avere una sua "patria nazionale" a cui poter fare ritorno. Di significato monumentale fu il riconoscimento ufficiale degli importantissimi legami *storici, religiosi e culturali* degli Ebrei con la terra dei loro padri, che sotto le dominazioni greca e romana divenne nota come "Palestina".

Poiché si trattava di una causa giusta e di un concetto giustificato, era necessario trovare un modo per elevare il contenuto di tale Dichiarazione a livello di legge internazionale. Di conseguenza, esso fu portato dal Consiglio Supremo delle Principali Potenze Alleate e Associate (Gran Bretagna, Francia, Italia, Giappone e Stati Uniti) alla Conferenza di Pace di Parigi nel 1919. La questione si fece più complessa man mano che venivano presentate richieste di rivendicazioni territoriali sia dalle delegazioni arabe che da quelle ebraiche, in quanto il vecchio Impero Ottomano stava per essere ripartito fra le potenze vincitrici; non fu quindi possibile risolvere la questione nel corso della Conferenza di Parigi.

Ciò che avvenne alla Conferenza di Parigi, e che contribuì alla progressione degli eventi che stiamo qui esaminando, fu la creazione della *Società delle Nazioni* che, all'Articolo 22 del suo Patto, prevedeva la costituzione di un sistema di mandati fiduciari sui territori del vecchio Impero Ottomano.

La successiva importante pietra miliare sul percorso verso uno status giuridico internazionale e una patria nazionale ebraica fu la *Conferenza di Sanremo*, tenutasi presso la Villa Devachan a Sanremo, in Italia, dal 18 al 26 aprile 1920. Si trattava di un'estensione' della Conferenza di Pace di Parigi del 1919, al fine di trattare alcune di queste questioni rimaste in sospeso. Lo scopo dei quattro (su cinque) membri del Consiglio delle Principali Potenze Alleate e Associate che si riunì a Sanremo (in quanto gli Stati Uniti erano presenti solo come osservatori, a motivo della politica non intervenzionista del Presidente Woodrow Wilson), consistette nel valutare le rivendicazioni presentate, deliberare e prendere decisioni sul riconoscimento legale di ciascuna rivendicazione. L'esito, sulla base dell'Articolo 22 del Patto della Società delle Nazioni, fu l'istituzione di tre mandati, uno su Siria e Libano (in seguito separato in due mandati), uno sulla Mesopotamia (Iraq), e uno sulla Palestina. Il *Mandato per la Palestina* fu affidato alla Gran Bretagna, come "impegno sacro per la civiltà" in relazione alla "costituzione in Palestina di un focolare nazionale per il popolo ebraico". Si trattava di una risoluzione giuridicamente vincolante di diritto internazionale.

In due dei tre mandati originali si riconosceva che il popolo indigeno aveva la capacità di autogovernarsi, con la potenza mandataria incaricata semplicemente di prestare assistenza nella costituzione di istituzioni di governo, ove necessario. Ciò non valeva per la Palestina, poiché essa, in base ai termini del Mandato, doveva diventare la patria ("focolare nazionale") del popolo ebraico. Nonostante il popolo ebraico fosse parte della popolazione indigena della Palestina, la maggioranza di esso all'epoca non viveva ancora in questa Terra. Il mandato per la Palestina era quindi molto diverso dagli altri e definiva come gli Ebrei si sarebbero stanziati nella Terra per poi formare una nazione realizzabile entro il territorio allora noto come "Palestina". Gli obblighi *singolari* del Mandato nei confronti del popolo ebraico in relazione allo stabilimento della loro patria nazionale in Palestina diedero pertanto un carattere *sui generis* (unico, singolare) al Mandato per la Palestina.

I confini della "Palestina" a cui si faceva riferimento nelle rivendicazioni presentate, includevano territori a *ovest e a est* del fiume Giordano. Le richieste degli Ebrei specificavano che il fine ultimo del Mandato sarebbe stato "la creazione di un commonwealth autonomo", beninteso che "nulla deve essere fatto che possa pregiudicare i diritti civili e religiosi delle comunità non ebraiche esistenti in Palestina". Il risultante Mandato per la Palestina, approvato dal Consiglio della Società delle Nazioni nel luglio del 1922, fu un trattato internazionale e come tale legalmente vincolante.

La decisione presa a Sanremo rappresentò uno spartiacque nella storia del popolo ebraico, che era stato un popolo senza patria per circa duemila anni. Dalla prospettiva di Chaim Weizmann, presidente della neonata Organizzazione Sionista e futuro primo Presidente dello Stato di Israele, "il riconoscimento dei nostri diritti in Palestina è incorporato nel trattato con la Turchia ed è divenuto parte del diritto internazionale. Questo rappresenta l'evento politico più rilevante in tutta la storia del nostro movimento, e forse non è esagerato dire in tutta la storia del nostro popolo a partire dall'Esilio." Secondo l'Organizzazione Sionista d'America, la Risoluzione di Sanremo "corona la dichiarazione britannica [Balfour] promulgandola come parte della legge delle nazioni del mondo".

La politica da implementare, come contenuta nel Mandato per la Palestina, era coerente con la Dichiarazione Balfour nel riconoscere in maniera significativa i legami di natura *storica, culturale e religiosa* del popolo ebraico con la Terra Santa e ancora più forte rispetto alla Dichiarazione a motivo dell'inserimento del principio fondamentale secondo cui la Palestina avrebbe dovuto essere *ricostituita* come focolare nazionale del popolo ebraico. È particolarmente importante sottolineare l'inclusione nei termini del Mandato (tramite l'Articolo 2) del principio fondamentale indicato nel Preambolo di questo accordo internazionale, secondo cui "con ciò è stato dato riconoscimento alla connessione storica del popolo ebreo con la Palestina e alle basi per ricostituire la loro nazione in quel paese".

L'obiettivo primario del Mandato era quello di provvedere *una patria nazionale al popolo ebraico*, incluso il popolo ebraico disperso *in tutto il mondo*, nella loro patria ancestrale. Al popolo arabo, che già esercitava la propria sovranità in un certo numero di stati, veniva garantita la protezione dei diritti civili e religiosi in forza del Mandato fino a quando desiderassero restare, anche dopo la formazione dello Stato di Israele nel 1948.

Inoltre, la Cisgiordania venne aggiunta nel frattempo ai territori sotto sovranità araba, *sottratta* dai Britannici *all'esatto territorio mandatario in questione*, prima della firma del Mandato stesso nel 1922 (v. di seguito).

Quando il Consiglio della Società delle Nazioni approvò il Mandato per la Palestina nel luglio del 1922, esso divenne vincolante per tutti i 51 membri della Società. Questo atto della Società consentì il realizzarsi del sogno a lungo accarezzato della *restaurazione del popolo ebraico nella loro antica terra e convalidò l'esistenza di fatti ed eventi storici che collegano il popolo ebraico alla Palestina*. Per il Consiglio Supremo delle Principali Potenze Alleate e per il Cosiglio della Società delle Nazioni, questi *fatti storici* furono considerati come *accettati e stabiliti*. Nelle parole di Neville Barbour: *"Nel 1922, la Dichiarazione Balfour fu sancita a livello internazionale attraverso l'istituzione del Mandato per la Palestina"*.

I diritti concessi al popolo ebraico nel Mandato per la Palestina dovevano avere efficacia in *tutta la Palestina*. Da ciò consegue che i *diritti legali* dei richiedenti sovranità sulla *Città vecchia di Gerusalemme* derivano analogamente dalle decisioni del Consiglio Supremo delle Principali Potenze Alleate a Sanremo e dai termini del Mandato per la Palestina approvato dal Consiglio della Società delle Nazioni.

Nel marzo del 1921, al Cairo, la Gran Bretagna decise di ripartire il territorio mandatario della Palestina per ragioni di politica internazionale proprie. L'Articolo 25 del Mandato conferiva alla Potenza Mandataria il permesso di posticipare o non applicare la maggior parte delle clausole del Mandato nell'area di terra ad est del fiume Giordano ("Cisgiordania"). La Gran Bretagna, in quanto Potenza Mandataria, esercitò tale diritto.

Per il professor Yehuda Zvi Blum, ex ambasciatore delle Nazioni Unite, *i diritti conferiti al popolo arabo della Palestina in relazione al principio dell'autodeterminazione vennero garantiti come conseguenza di tale iniziale partizione della Palestina approvata dal Consiglio della Società delle Nazioni nel 1922*. Secondo il professor Blum: *"Gli Arabi palestinesi godono da lungo tempo dell'autodeterminazione nel proprio stato, lo Stato arabo palestinese della Giordania"*. (Vale la pena sottolineare che, in una lettera scritta probabilmente il 17 gennaio 1921 al segretario privato di Churchill, il Col. T. E. Lawrence ("d'Arabia") segnalava che, in cambio della sovranità araba in Iraq, Cisgiordania e Siria, il figlio maggiore di Re

Hussein, l'Emiro Feisal, uomo noto secondo Lawrence per la fedeltà alle proprie promesse, aveva "*acconsentito ad abbandonare qualsiasi rivendicazione paterna nei confronti della Palestina*".)

Dopo questa partizione, Churchill, all'epoca Segretario Coloniale britannico, riaffermò immediatamente l'impegno della Gran Bretagna a conferire efficacia alle politiche della Dichiarazione Balfour in *tutte le altre parti del territorio* coperto dal Mandato per la Palestina a ovest del fiume Giordano. *L'impegno era riferito anche all'area di Gerusalemme e della sua Città Vecchia.* Nelle parole di Churchill: "È palesemente giusto che gli Ebrei, che sono sparsi in tutto il mondo, debbano avere una sede nazionale e un focolare nazionale dove alcuni di loro possano essere riuniti. E dove altro potrebbe essere se non nella terra di Palestina, con la quale sono stati intimamente e profondamente associati per oltre tremila anni?"

Quindi, in breve, le *fondamenta primarie del diritto internazionale per la rivendicazione "legale" basata sui "diritti storici" o sul "titolo storico" del popolo ebraico in riferimento alla Palestina sono le decisioni di Sanremo dell'aprile 1920, il Mandato per la Palestina del luglio 1922,* approvato dal Consiglio della Società delle Nazioni e firmato dalle stesse Principali Forze Alleate e divenuto quindi un trattato internazionale vincolante per tutti gli Stati Membri, *e lo stesso Patto della Società delle Nazioni (Art. 22).*

Parte II: La Questione di una Dichiarazione Unilaterale di

uno Stato di Palestina

Trascorsero molti anni dall'adozione del Mandato nel 1922 alla creazione dello Stato di Israele nel 1948. Un evento che accelerò la creazione dello Stato di Israele fu il voto dell'Assemblea Generale delle Nazioni Unite nel 1947 per la partizione della Palestina (Risoluzione 181 (II)), raccomandando l'istituzione di uno Stato Ebraico e di uno Stato Arabo in quel territorio. Sebbene le risoluzioni dell'Assemblea Generale delle Nazioni Unite abbiano una valenza pari esclusivamente a raccomandazioni e non siano dunque legalmente vincolanti, gli Ebrei accettarono il piano di partizione, mentre gli Arabi lo rigettarono. Il Regno Unito di Gran Bretagna rinuncio' al suo ruolo di Mandatario e si ritiro' dal territorio il 14 maggio 1948. Quello stesso giorno, con effetto dalla mezzanotte, gli Ebrei dichiararono lo Stato di Israele.

Il giorno seguente, gli eserciti di cinque nazioni arabe circostanti attaccarono immediatamente il nuovo Stato Ebraico (Guerra d'Indipendenza d'Israele). GliArabi vennero inaspettatamente sconfitti. La Giordania, tuttavia, annesse illegalmente la Giudea e la Samaria. Israele riacquisto' il controllo del suo territorio di mandato nel corso di una guerra di auto-difesa, la Guerra dei Sei Giorni, nel 1967. Nonostante tali eventi abbiano influenzato la rilevanza del Mandato, in modo particolare avendo portato alla realizzazione del suo scopo primario, la creazione di uno Stato Ebraico, alcuni aspetti fondamentali del Mandato rimangono validi e legalmente vincolanti, e sono estremamente rilevanti per la determinazione delle "questioni chiave" che devono essere negoziate fra le due parti circa lo "status permanente" (o "status finale") di Gerusalemme e della "Cisgiordania/West Bank".

Al fine di ottenere la giusta prospettiva nel considerare l'ambito legale internazionale in cui si inserisce la questione di uno Stato palestinese dichiarato tale a livello unilaterale, con la parte orientale di Gerusalemme come capitale, potremmo aver bisogno di andare oltre la legge, *per se*, al fine di tenere conto dell'impatto dell'opinione pubblica sulla formulazione delle consuetudini legali e delle leggi internazionali codificate. Di conseguenza, bisognerebbe attrarre l'attenzione al livello in cui le risoluzioni eque ai "problemi principali" dell'odierno conflitto israeliano/arabo palestinese possano essere esacerbate da iperboli linguistiche, distorsioni dei fatti o manovre puramente politiche e calcolata retorica. Parte della retorica risente dell'esigenza critica di essere esposta alla luce della terminologia e precisione legale, altrimenti può facilmente portare a una crassa distorsione della verità, che può dare luogo persino a risposte legali internazionali sconsiderate.

Prendiamo per esempio l'*identità "palestinese"*. Al momento della decisione di Sanremo e del risultante Mandato per la Palestina, il territorio allora noto come "Palestina" venne designato espressamente per la "*ricostituzione*" del "focolare nazionale" del popolo ebraico *soltanto*. Mentre erano state intraprese debite misure per proteggere i diritti degli Arabi e degli altri abitanti, solo gli Ebrei erano un popolo rimasto senza una patria. Questo era in realtà lo scopo precipuo del Mandato per la Palestina e il suo predecessore, la Dichiarazione Balfour. Al momento del Mandato, sarebbe stato più preciso fare riferimento agli "Ebrei palestinesi" e agli "Arabi palestinesi" (insieme ad altri abitanti non ebrei), ma a motivo della creazione dello Stato di Israele, gli Ebrei palestinesi mantennero il loro antico nome di "Israeliani" mentre i non ebrei (principalmente, ma non tutti, arabi) si appropriarono del nome di "Palestinesi", con il risultato di essere spesso erroneamente considerati come i legittimi abitanti del territorio. In realtà, la terra denominata "Palestina" copre un territorio denominato dagli Ebrei "Terra Santa" molto prima che il nome "Palestina" fosse utilizzato per la prima volta da Greci e Romani. La verità è che il territorio un tempo noto come "Palestina" non è mai stato, né dal momento in cui tale nome venne utilizzato né prima, una nazione araba, ovvero non è mai stato designato come nazione araba. Questa nomenclatura, tuttavia, apporta un forte impatto psicologico con l'inferenza che i precedenti abitanti arabi della Palestina sarebbero i *veri* "Palestinesi" e che essi *soltanto* fanno parte della "Palestina".

Per quanto riguarda la *questione dei rifugiati,* la definizione legale di "rifugiato" è la seguente: "una persona che fugge o viene espulsa da una nazione, soprattutto a causa di persecuzione e cerca riparo in un'altra nazione" (Black's Law Dictionary). L'attuale difficile situazione di coloro che vivono nei campi dei rifugiati è davvero deplorevole ed evoca giustamente la compassione del mondo, ma la maggior parte dei Palestinesi identificati come "rifugiati" sono distanti più di una generazione dagli eventi che causarono la fuga della generazione precedente. A vaste aree di terra araba fu concessa l'indipendenza generazioni fa e poterono facilmente accogliere tutti questi sfortunati "rifugiati" che sono diventati uno spettacolo per sei decenni invece di integrarsi come membri produttivi della società fra la loro gente. *In aggiunta* agli altri territori del Mandato di Sanremo che ottennero la condizione di Stato prima di Israele, e avrebbero potuto facilmente assorbire i loro fratelli arabi, la Cisgiordania fu ripartita *appositamente* per gli Arabi palestinesi all'interno del territorio originariamente destinato al focolare nazionale ebraico. *Ciò fornì già un 'nuovo Stato' legittimo agli Arabi entro il territorio della "Palestina".* Il diritto internazionale non ha mai dovuto cimentarsi con la questione dell'ereditarietà' dello status di rifugiato, e tale situazione è divenuta unica nella storia umana.

Per quanto riguarda le *"linee del 1967",* come punto di riferimento per un nuovo potenziale Stato palestinese, esiste una menzione costante di ritiro entro i *"confini del 1967".* Prima di tutto questa terminologia è legalmente scorretta. Il termine "confini" viene generalmente utilizzato nella giurisprudenza internazionale per indicare dei "confini nazionali", cosa che le "linee" del 1967 sicuramente non sono. La giurisprudenza internazionale definisce come "confine" "una delimitazione fra una nazione (o una suddivisione politica [di tale nazione]) e un'altra" (Black's Law Dictionary). Tali confini nazionali non sono mai stati stabiliti per il rinato Stato di Israele. Le "linee" del 1967 sono linee puramente *militari* di non attraversamento ("linee di demarcazione di armistizio"), derivanti dalla Guerra di Indipendenza di Israele del 1948. E' stato *espressamente* ribadito nel corso dei *numerosi* accordi di armistizio del 1949 tra Israeliani e Palestinesi, che queste "linee" né rappresentano confini nazionali, né pregiudicano la futura negoziazione bilaterale degli stessi. Queste linee di armistizio del 1949 restarono valide fino allo scoppio della Guerra dei Sei Giorni nel 1967. Collegarle alla guerra del 1967, in cui il territorio perduto venne recuperato dalle forze di difesa israeliane, sotto attacco, chiamandole i "confini del 1967" invece che le linee di armistizio del 1949, favorisce l'errata nozione che si tratti di "confini" illeciti, compromettendo profondamente la questione e i suoi esiti. Eugene Rostow, Sottosegretario di Stato statunitense per gli Affari Politici nel 1967, nonché uno degli autori della *Risoluzione 242* del Consiglio Nazionale per la Sicurezza delle Nazioni Unite del 1967 relativa a confini "sicuri e protetti", affermò nel 1990 che tale Risoluzione e la successiva Risoluzione 338 del Consiglio di Sicurezza "…si basano su due principi: Israele può gestire il territorio fino a quando i suoi vicini arabi non faranno la pace e quando la pace sarà fatta Israele dovrà ritirarsi entro 'confini sicuri e riconosciuti', che non devono necessariamente essere gli stessi delle Linee di demarcazione dell'armistizio del 1949". In altri termini, le linee del 1967 *non* sono affatto "confini", e questo termine non dev'essere utilizzato per creare e perpetuare l'impressione che Israele abbia illegalmente trasgredito i confini di un altro Stato, quando non è affatto così.

Analogamente, per quanto riguarda i *territori disputati*, l'uso diffuso dei termini "territori occupati" invece che "territori disputati" (cosa che corrisponde alla realtà) ha un enorme impatto psicologico che può dare luogo a ramificazioni reali e persino legali. Inoltre, questo linguaggio e ciò che tende a connotare ("occupazione belligerante") ignorano totalmente il linguaggio del trattato internazionale, che utilizza il termine "*ricostituito*", così come contenuto nel Mandato per la Palestina. Il territorio *ricostituito* preclude un'"occupazione belligerante", anche se i confini nazionali permanenti devono ancora essere negoziati.

Uno Stato non può, per definizione, essere una "potenza di occupazione belligerante" in un territorio che viene "ricostituito" nel proprio nome, secondo le norme di uno strumento legalmente vincolante di diritto internazionale. L'"occupazione si verifica quando uno Stato belligerante invade il territorio di un altro Stato con l'intenzione di mantenere tale territorio almeno temporaneamente" (West's Encyclopedia of American Law). Il territorio reclamato da Israele nel 1967 non è mai stato legittimamente "il territorio di un altro Stato", né Israele lo ha ottenuto con una guerra di aggressione. Esso in realtà era un territorio specificatamente designato per un focolare nazionale *ebraico*, secondo il Mandato per la Palestina legalmente vincolante del 1922.

Uno stretto corollario a tutto ciò è rappresentato dalla questione degli *insediamenti*. La delicatezza di tale questione è esacerbata dal fatto che la legalità/illegalità di tali insediamenti si basa su fattori che potrebbero non seguire norme prescritte di diritto internazionale, ma che sono di fatto complicati dalla natura unica del caso di Israele. Per esempio, spesso si afferma che tali insediamenti violano l'Articolo 49 della Convenzione di Ginevra (IV), ma l'inclusione di tale articolo nella Convenzione aveva uno scopo ben diverso da quello di governare circostanze come quelle esistenti nell'odierna Israele. L'intento degli autori era quello di *proteggere i civili vulnerabili in tempi di conflitti armati,* creando uno strumento legale internazionale che avrebbe dichiarato illegittima qualsiasi *deportazione coatta* come quella sofferta da oltre quaranta milioni di tedeschi, sovietici, polacchi, ucraini, ungheresi e altri, subito dopo la Seconda Guerra Mondiale. Nel caso di Israele, in base alla legislazione internazionale, così come rappresentata dal Mandato per la Palestina, agli Ebrei non solo veniva *permesso* di insediarsi in *ogni parte* della Palestina, erano addirittura *incoraggiati* a farlo, *non* venivano però deportati o trasferiti con la forza dal governo. Di conseguenza, chiamare "illegali" gli insediamenti israeliani di "Gerusalemme est", della Giudea e della Samaria non è un'applicazione appropriata della Quarta Convenzione di Ginevra.

La *questione di Gerusalemme* è forse la più volatile di tutte. A motivo della sacralità di questa Città per molti, è diventato evidente che le posizioni di Israele e Palestinesi riguardo alla Città Vecchia sono a tutti gli effetti irriconciliabili. La prova di questo fatto è che essa non fu nominata nel Framework for Peace (Quadro per la Pace) in Medioriente, adottato negli Accordi di Camp David del 1978 fra

Israele ed Egitto. In quest'ultimo caso, Gerusalemme era in realtà inclusa nell'ordine del giorno ma fu lasciata fuori dai veri e propri accordi a causa dell'incapacità delle due parti di risolvere le loro fondamentali discrepanze su questa seria questione. Il fallimento del Summit di Camp David del luglio 2000 sottolineò ancora una volta il significato della questione di Gerusalemme e della Città Vecchia.

Arrivando al *ruolo delle Nazioni Unite* nel corrente dibattito, bisogna ricordare che, secondo la Carta delle Nazioni Unite, l'Assemblea Generale delle Nazioni Unite non ha il potere di creare decisioni legalmente vincolanti. Le Risoluzioni dell'Assemblea Generale possono solo raccomandare, ma non hanno forza vincolante.

Pertanto, anche se si dovesse arrivare ad una Risoluzione che "riconoscesse" gli "Arabi palestinesi" quale entità politica/Stato, ciò non costituirebbe, di per sé, la creazione di uno Stato di Palestina ai sensi della legislazione internazionale, non più di quanto la Risoluzione 181 (II) (il Piano di Partizione delle Nazioni Unite) del 1947 abbia creato lo Stato di Israele.

Inoltre, entrambe le parti si sono impegnate a seguire la via dei negoziati per arrivare ad uno *"status permanente"*. La leadership dell'OLP promise nel 1993 di affidare ai *negoziati* la risoluzione di praticamente *tutte* le questioni importanti relative allo "status permanente". A norma dell'Accordo ad interim (Oslo II) del 1995, le parti si impegnarono a *non agire unilateralmente* per modificare lo status dei territori prima di aver raggiunto risultati attraverso i negoziati sullo status permanente. Venne chiaramente statuito e concordato che: "...*nessuna delle parti* avrebbe iniziato o intrapreso *alcun passo* che *modificasse lo status* della Cisgiordania e della striscia di Gaza prima dei risultati dei *negoziati sullo status permanente"*.

Una dichiarazione unilaterale dello Stato Palestinese sarebbe pertanto in violazione dell'impegno preso ed espresso in uno strumento legale internazionale, come anche in dichiarazioni pubbliche e documenti ufficiali e pubblicati.

Per riassumere, il conflitto non è un conflitto tradizionale sui *confini*. Questo non è neanche il vero problema, come dimostra il fatto che i confini rimangono fino a questo momento indeterminati. Si tratta di un conflitto sui diritti storici e sul bisogno, riconosciuto a livello internazionale, di un 'popolo' unificato ad ottenere un proprio posto (e spazio territoriale) dove poter tornare a 'casa' dopo duemila anni di 'apolidia' e separazione dalla Terra dei loro padri, *l'unico* posto che definiscono "santo" e l'*unica* Terra che abbiano mai chiamato "patria".

ABOUT THE AUTHOR

DR. CYNTHIA DAY Wallace received her PhD in international law from Cambridge University (UK) under Professor Sir Derek Bowett (Queen's Counsel and, *inter alia*, General Counsel for the United Nations Relief and Works Agency for Palestine Refugees in the Near East (UNRWA), Beirut 1966–68). Dr. Wallace's international law career spans some thirty years, including academic and senior diplomatic-level posts, among which Deputy Executive Director, Investment Negotiation Program, International Law Institute, Georgetown University Law Center, Washington DC; Senior Fellow and Project Director, International Business and Economics Program, Center for Strategic and International Studies (CSIS), Washington DC ("think tank"); and Senior Adviser to the Executive Secretary, United Nations Economic Commission for Europe (ECE), Geneva (diplomatic-level post). With more than thirty publications (including six books), she is the recipient of the Grotius International Law Award for a law journal article selected jointly by the U.N. Association and the T.M.C. Asser Institute of The Hague. She is a U.S. citizen and resides in Geneva, Switzerland.

CONTACT THE AUTHOR

All comments welcomed, through the publisher or by
e-mailing cdwallace@bluewin.ch.

ACKNOWLEDGMENTS

THE AUTHOR WOULD like to acknowledge the following individuals who have made meaningful contributions to the realization of the present book. The original research for the present book was carried out at the Max Planck Institute for Comparative Public Law and International Law in Heidelberg, Germany, at the generous invitation of the Directors, Professor Dr. Armin von Bogdandy and Professor Dr. H.C. Rüdiger Wolfrum. My thanks then go out to those who read the content and responded with constructive comments and welcome feedback on the early drafts. First, to Jacques Gauthier whose introduction—over lunch 'coincidentally' in the very same hotel in Geneva (*Les Bergues*) that housed the French delegation at the historic First Assembly of the League of Nations over ninety years earlier—to his monumental study of the historical, religious, political and legal aspects of the Old City of Jerusalem laid the solid historical foundations for Part I of the present book, and who clarified certain factual anomalies that came from less thoroughly researched secondary sources. Next, my admiration and gratitude go to Elizabeth Allan whose tireless fine-tuning of the many behind-the-scenes intricacies and fine points of history and history-in-the-making brought various aspects of the historical and modern-day drama alive and earned her the title of my "London walking archive", faithful and committed to the last jot and tittle, sharing with me numerous very long nights with tireless exchanges, at times between totally different time zones, extending our clocks at both ends, giving of herself to the very end. I am also indebted to those others who read and responded with bits and pieces of their own existential knowledge, and/or even lending painstaking proofreading skills, that all went to make up parts of the overall fabric woven together into the present treatise, some directing me to their own writings on, or bordering on, the focus of the content. These include Eli Herz, Roy Thurley, Solomon Benzimra and Pieter Bos. Enormous gratitude also goes out to Katariina Salmi who helped to round up just the right godly translators willing to generously contribute their time and talents to see that accurate summaries would be available to people of other nations and tongues. These include Gregory Lafitte (French), Monica Tamagnini (Italian), and Magdalena Paulus and Hanspeter Buechi (German), all of whom made meaningful retouches and revisions to the original translations. And without Katariina's help in gathering photos, the book would simply have had no pictures. She and I are both grateful for the kind cooperation of Alfredo Moreschi and Alessandro Perotti in San Remo, Italy, who provided the San Remo masterpiece of 'the greats', as well as United Nations Archivist Jacques Oberson who guided us through the League of Nations collection and offered *carte blanche* whatever photo(s) we might choose, standing by to help us gain direct access for the best results.

Katariina helped as well with other logistics and technical matters in earlier phases of the project when this book was yet in the form of a less-developed document, at which stage also Paul Tielens lent his amazing technical skills, with an eternally patient and utterly gracious 11th- (read: 12th)-hour readiness—producing admirably and impeccably formatted and harmonized documents, complete with foreign language supplements, always just in time, owing to my final-hour 'photo finishes', and always in a true heart of service and exemplary professionalism, with a human touch.

The Foreword speaks for itself as regards Tomas Sandell who transmitted to me this vision one God-ordained day by the Lake of Geneva, with no idea at the time where this was ultimately going to lead. Tomas is a Joseph—one man tirelessly and selflessly taking on a monumental task to do his part to save a nation. It is an honor to have been prepared by God to partner with Tomas in this amazing and timely endeavor to bring the message of the San-Remo-based international legal rights of the Jewish people and the State of Israel to the attention of the world.

To all of the above, and any others whose names I may have missed but whom God has seen and whose names He has written in heaven, I owe a debt of gratitude. Above all, without the Holy Spirit, I could never have had the insights or the 24/7 endurance to see this sensitive and urgent aspect of the mission through to its completion. Still, I know that this is only the beginning; the fruits are yet to come; and you are all a part of the future harvest.

Lord Balfour, Prime Minister of UK 1902–1905, Foreign Secretary 1916–1919

1ère session du Conseil, présidée par M. Léon Bourgeois (France)
Paris, 16 Janv. 1920.

First Session of the Council of the League of Nations, Paris, January 1920

Leaders of the Principal Allied Powers at Villa Devachan, San Remo, Italy, April 1920

Temple Mount area, Jerusalem today